SATURDAY AND SUNDAY

SATURDAY AND SUNDAY

BY

EDMUND KEMPER BROADUS

Essay Index Reprint Series

BOOKS FOR LIBRARIES PRESS, INC.
FREEPORT, NEW YORK

Originally published by:

THE MACMILLAN COMPANY OF
CANADA LIMITED

First published 1935
Reprinted 1967

PRINTED IN THE UNITED STATES OF AMERICA

TO

HENRY MARSHALL TORY

First President of the University of Alberta,
this little book is affectionately dedicated

FOREWORD

I came to Alberta in 1908 to share in the building up of a provincial university in a sparsely-settled province which had only just been carved out of the Northwest Territories. I had spent the immediately preceding years at Harvard. The abrupt change from that age-old tradition to educational pioneering in the Canadian northwest accounts for a certain *naïveté* which I find now in these early impressions. They are I think, a little overwrought —"tenderfoot" impressions, at which a real pioneer would tolerantly smile. But I have resuscitated them, and left them substantially unchanged, with the thought that, after all, the development, under such conditions, of a provincial university of respectable size and rank, is not a common thing; and that people who are accustomed to taking universities for granted, may find these early impressions interesting.

The rest of the essays deal with books and men of letters. Writing them has been a week-end diversion, a Saturday-Sunday interlude, in the routine of teaching. I rescue them—or at least such few as seem worth rescuing—from the bygone pages of the *Atlantic Monthly,* the *London Mercury,* Andrew McPhail's *University Magazine* (now, alas, defunct), and sundry other periodicals, in the hope that, because I had good fun writing them, the indulgent reader (if the animal exists) may have some fun reading them.

E. K. B.

October, 1935.

ACKNOWLEDGMENTS

The publishers desire to acknowledge the aid given by the University of Alberta, through the committee which administers the Carnegie Corporation Research Grant, toward the publication of this book.

Grateful acknowledgment is made to *The Atlantic Monthly* for "At the End of the Line" (May, 1910), "At the End of the Line in War Time" (Feb. 1916), "The Preface" (Jan. 1906), "The Armoury: A Fantasy" (Contributors' Club), and "Genius at School" (Feb. 1914); to Sir Andrew Macphail and *The University Magazine* for "A Simple Person" (originally published under the title: "William Caxton: Simple Person" April, 1913), and "An Old Book Shelf" (Feb. 1910); to *The Dalhousie Review* for "An Elizabethan Diarist" (1923); to The Clarendon Press for "Dear Fine Silly Old Angel" (originally published as an "Introduction" to Selections from Thomas Fuller); to *The London Mercury* for "Mr. Richardson Arrives" (Sept. 1933) and "The Laureateship" (June, 1930)—title changed to "Official Poets"; to the *University of California Chronicle* for "A Diplomatic Appraisal" (Vol. XVII, No. 4); and to *The Canadian Medical Association Journal* for "Medicine and English Literature" (October, 1912).

CONTENTS

I

II

III

I

AT THE END OF THE LINE

I

THERE has always been a seductive magic to me in the railway track. As a child I would follow those long, remotely-converging lines of steel, in the hope of finding at last the meeting-point of the infinitely elongated V; and the fact that not even my occasional rides on the train ever brought me to it, and that from the rear of an observation-car the meeting-point of the rails seemed somehow to have slipped in behind us without our passing over it,—this came to be classed with the end of the rainbow as a part of the natural magic of which the queer world seemed so full. And since I have grown to man's estate, the track has still lured me with its uncompromising directness in the face of the deviousness of nature, and with the sense of the indestructibility of the bond by which the unceasing steel links settlement and distant settlement together.

To my earlier and in a sense to my later experience, as well, the most impressive fact of the rails was that they never stopped. Dweller as I was, sometimes in small towns and sometimes in the country, the train seemed to thunder down that infinite parallel and pause for a moment beside the little station and the telegraph-tower and the water-tank, only to go on to infinity again. And this sense, as it were, of the both-way infinity of the line came to be not only its most impressive, but also its most characteristic and inalienable, quality.

And then suddenly, not long ago, all the old anchors of experience were lifted or broken, and the train bore me out of my familiar haunts, out of my native country, over the Canadian border, and ever westward and northward on and on to a point whither the insatiable adventure-lust of man had pushed the frontier of civilization. And there the train stopped and I got out. There was nothing else to do. It was the end of the line.

Only gradually did the full significance of this fact dawn upon me. At first, life was blurred with detail. I saw too much to see anything. But slowly, as the process of adjustment went on, it became clear that the key to the new life on which I had entered, the explanation of this sense of *difference* which time and experience were proving powerless to diminish, lay in the fact that we were all living and working and thinking and feeling at the end of the line. This realization came to me first through the perception that the arrival and the departure of trains was not an incident. It was an event. The old boyhood lure of the train re-turned; but now it was not due to the dim con-sciousness of a both-way infinity,—

"Into this Universe and Why not knowing
Nor Whence. . . ."

Rather had I reached a spot where the line had at
once its end and its beginning. When the train
came in and stopped with the finality which was at
first so strange to me, I could see with the eye of
recollection what the disembarking passengers had
just been through—the day after day of journey
over the prairie, the semi-occasional stop at a point
where a grain-elevator and a cluster of houses
marked the nucleus of settlement, the glimpse now
and then of the red coat of a Royal Northwest
Mounted Policeman as he paced his hundred-mile
"beat". I could recall too the thrill of a certain
moment when the train was passing a lonely cabin
on the prairie, and the denizen of the little cabin
had stepped to his door and waved to the passing
train—had waved not with the turn of the wrist
to which I was accustomed, but with a long, slow
sweep of the full arm which somehow reflected the
limitless prairie round about him. These things
the new arrivals too had seen. They too were not
the casual traffickers of some near-by station, but,
like me, had sustained the unremitting journey of
many days to reach the strange new life where the
train came to a stop.

And so, too, with the starting of the train. These
men who swung aboard at the warning of the
whistle, to a chorus of farewells—these men were

to view the prairie for many days, until at last the
unending rails would bear them into a world becoming ever less spacious and more crowded,—
would bear them on and on until they were lost
somewhere in the swarming welter of the East.
But the train would never stop.

And thus, as I have said, it came to me out of
these daily arrivals and departures, these events
of the train which, however repeated, never lost
their significance, that the key to this new life lay
in the fact that it was at the end of the line. Everywhere in the day's work and in the day's play, at
the desk, in the shop, in the counting-house, on the
farm, one felt the underlying consciousness that
routine, tradition, the treadmill of blind habit, lay
back there in a country where the rails had already
passed. Back there, life was an accomplished fact,
a finished machine into which you must be content to fit as a cog into its groove. But here life
was in the making, still to be hammered into shape
and use. And you were not merely a cog. Instead,
you wielded the hammer. And so you bared your
arms with the feeling that you were in at the making of life, and that, in the casting off of the old
and the shaping of the new, you had found yourself.

II

But if the life lived here has a deeper significance,
it is not wanting either in picturesque details; and

these picturesque details, again, are implicit in the fact that here the railway ends. The magic of civilization which flows along these threads of steel has erected, with almost the abruptness of an Aladdin palace, a thriving city. On one side of the river which rolls down from the Rocky Mountains is rising a structure of granite and marble, which will house the legislative activities of the province. On the other side of the river, the ground is being broken for a group of buildings which will be the home of the Provincial University. Over the bridges which span the stream ply the trolley-cars; the business streets are alive with commerce, and the residence sections of the twin-cities blossom with dwellings. Law and order, wisdom and culture, industry and finance—these are the products of civilization, these are the result of the magic which flows along the lines of steel.

But cheek-by-jowl with these evidences of a highly developed life are evidences of the primitive world on the edge of which we dwell. The developed life is here because the railroad comes here. The primitive life is here because the railroad stops here. The one has taken the other by surprise.

This juxtaposition of extremes, this sense of contrast, finds its most effective symbol in a long low structure of whitewashed logs within a few rods of the Parliament building. The rambling two-storey log hut is the old Hudson's Bay Company fort, around which the early history of Edmonton centres. As early as 1795, the Hudson's Bay Company established a trading post here, and in 1820, the Fort was built. It was at that time the largest of the Company's structures west of York Factory. Around it stretched a palisade, twenty feet high and enclosing a court-yard three hundred feet long and two hundred and ten feet wide. At the four corners of the palisade were bastions from whose port holes cannon projected. When Sir George Simpson passed through Edmonton in 1841 on his "Overland Journey Round the World", he found the fort "decorated both inside and out with paintings and devices to suit the taste of the savages that frequent it. Over the gateways are a most fanciful variety of vanes; but the hall, of which both the ceiling and the walls present the gaudiest colours and the most fantastic sculpture, absolutely rivets the astonished natives to the spot with wonder and admiration."

In 1859, when Captain Palliser sojourned in the fort, there was a population of about one hundred souls ("twenty-seven men, nineteen women, forty-eight children") living in and around it; and what impressed the Captain most was the extraordinary amount of meat, "four hundred pounds of fresh buffalo meat per day(!)" which they consumed. Outside of the fort, the only activity in those days was a flour mill run by wind-power; its grinding stones had been made by splitting a crude granite block, and could be made to turn only "when they get a gale of wind".

In 1863 Viscount Milton (*The Northwest Passage by Land*) records that "the boats required for the annual voyage to York Factory in Hudson's Bay are built and mended here" and that wheat grows luxuriantly in the vicinity; but the population still consisted of "about thirty families".

In 1868, according to the old Methodist missionary, John McDougall, the stable population was still only about one hundred and fifty, but "outside its walls hundreds, sometimes thousands encamped. Hither the tribes came up for trade and barter, as also for war and revenge; here many a temporary peace was patched up and again broken; here scenes of butchery and rapine and murder took place, and it was truly wonderful how this stout little frontier post still held its own throughout the years, amidst such constant turbulence and strife."

From this period until the arrival of the railway Edmonton remained in the inchoate village stage. A few adventurous pioneers drifted out from Fort Garry (Winnipeg) and homesteaded near it. Wheat and small garden truck were cultivated after a fashion, but there was no market. The buffalo vanished. The Indians, always a lurking danger, became an immediate menace in the Riel rebellion, and the panic-stricken settlers crowded within the walls of the fort. When the Riel rebellion simmered down, the village settled back to its trapping, fur-trading, and truck-gardening once more.

Meanwhile, the nearest railway station remained Winnipeg, or Fort Garry, a thousand miles away. "Going to the station" (a phrase endeared as with a casual charm to those of us who remember a country boyhood) meant a three or four months' journey in a Red River cart. Gentle Reader, have you ever seen a Red River cart? Its body, set springless upon a single heavy thwart or axle bar, was borne upon two mighty, wooden wheels, whose felloes were broad enough to go *over* muskeg instead of sinking *into* it. Their creaking was as the wailing of the damned souls in Dante's *Inferno:*

> "Now 'gin the rueful wailings to be heard,
> Now am I come where many a plaining voice
> Smites on my ear."

You will still find men in the Northwest who recall long rides in that antique vehicle. They recall it now with an appearance of philosophic calm; but I refuse to believe that any man ever rode a thousand miles in a Red River cart and preserved his integrity. Not even the original Kentucky mule could have engendered profanity so varied and prolonged.

It will seem to you, perhaps, a far cry from the Red River cart to the railroad. But the astonishing thing is that instead of being a far cry it is such a

very short one. They almost overlap, indeed, this
itinerant torture-chamber of the past, and the
modern Pullman. Already the pioneer transcontinental, the Canadian Pacific, was moving slowly
westward. At length it passed two hundred miles
south of Edmonton and in due time sent a spur
northward to the little fort settlement on the edge
of the wilderness.

Meantime, the Northwest Territories had been
divided into provinces, and the Province of Alberta,
some four times as large as all the New England
states put together, had been brought into being.
Edmonton was made its capital; and beside the old
Fort, now shorn of its protective stockade, is rising
the substantial stone work of the Parliament building.

There are other such material contrasts also: the
wretched little shack wherein "school kept" a few
years ago, is only a ten-minutes' walk from the site
of the Provincial University; the Edmonton City
Club, with all the appointments of club luxury,
crowns a hill on the slope of which burrows a primitive dugout with its crude roof half-earthed in
the hillside; and tents, the mushroom growth of a
night, are interspersed on the residence-streets with
frame dwellings. Some of the tents too are enriched
with fine furnishings; while others, although the
flimsy walls must bear the fifty-degrees-below of
this far northern winter, lack even the bare neces-
saries of decent comfort. And as if purposely to

heighten the contrasts, a few of these primitive dwellings display the "shingle" of a manicurist or a *masseuse*.

Equally replete with contrasts is the passing throng on the streets. Englishmen, Scotchmen, Frenchmen, Americans, rub shoulders with the "silent smoky Indian". Not infrequently, indeed, the contrast of costume is even more sharply drawn, when in the bitter winter the "tailor-made" man follows the example of his copper brother and dons the warm moccasin instead of the unyielding and unprotecting shoe of civilization. The trap drawn by the high-stepping hackney crowds the primitive ox-cart on the thoroughfares. Within the department stores, with their varied equipment, the woman of *ton* shops side by side with the Indian squaw and the swarthy half-breed woman of the prairies. The Indian leaves his ox-cart to take his first ride on a trolley-car; and the immigrant, bringing his numerous family into the same conveyance, shrewdly essays a "dicker" with the conductor for wholesale rates on his large consignment of passengers.

It was on the very trolley-ride on which I witnessed this futile effort at striking a bargain, that I saw an even more typical instance of the extremes which meet at the end of the line. A rough, unkempt, and rather malodorous person, whose speech betrayed the recency of his transplanting from the central European "mother-country", handed me an envelope, and asked me to direct him to the address upon it. I recognized the address at once as the residence of a man of culture whose daughter had just taken her degree at an eastern college. The immigrant, it appeared, had recently been appointed a "school trustee" of the district in which he lived. The daughter of the gentleman whose address was on the letter was in search of local experience as a public-school teacher. She had answered an advertisement from this district; and in response this uncouth trustee had journeyed to the city to inspect the applicant. The young lady, I knew, was shy, refined, totally inexperienced in "roughing it". What an experience was in store for her! Difficult—but how salutary it might be for both parties to the compact!

III

It is such incidents as these that keep one constantly reminded of the fact that this is the end of the line. But far more stimulating to the imagination, if less a matter of everyday experience, are the occasional reminders that, beyond this point where the line ends, stretch the "silent places", the *terra incognita* of the Farther North. Turn to the maps, even the most recent ones, of the Province of Alberta, and compare the wealth of detail concerning the country over which the steel stretches, with the meagre information beyond the point where the steel ends. What a sense of un-

fathomed mystery, of unplumbed depths, of un-
mounted heights, in this Northland! Less and less
grow the records as your finger follows the broad
band of the province northward. And when you
reach its northern boundary, you find yourself on
the edge of a country in which facts vanish altogether, and uncertainty wavers to an interrogation
point.

Does it not give you a vivid sense of "the little
done, the undone vast", to learn that our knowledge to-day of the great tract lying between Great
Slave Lake (just north of Alberta) and Dubawnt
Lake, far to the eastward, is gained from the
recorded wanderings of an eighteenth-century explorer, Samuel Hearne—his casual jottings—and
nothing else? And to be here at the end of the line
is to be in some sense a sharer in this mystery, this
lure of the unknown.

For here, as in the past, still come the swarthy
trappers with their season's gleanings, every pelt an
item in the record of hardship and adventure. *Pro
pelle cutem* reads the stern motto on the coat of
arms of the Hudson's Bay Company; and all the
willingness of the hardy adventurer to barter comfort and safety, and life itself, for the priceless fur
is suggested in that pregnant phrase. Here they
come, these veterans of the wild, here to the end
of the line. And from here, too, set out the men
who have hearkened to

"One everlasting Whisper, day and night re-
      peated—so:
'Something hidden. Go and find it. Go and
      look behind the Ranges—
Something lost behind the Ranges. Lost and
      waiting for you. Go!'"

And listening to the Everlasting Whisper, they go
to explore the Unknown for the pure joy of discovery.

From here, too, go the mails for the remote posts
and forts in the Farther North—to the nearer ones
as often as every few weeks, but to the farther ones,
only twice a year; and these goings if they are a
mere incident to the careless sojourner at the end
of the line, are surely an epoch to him who can see
in spirit the eager hearts in those distant lonely
posts.

From here, too, in the feverish Klondike days
which have passed into history, the gold-seekers
outfitted and started on their long journey. The
men who lived here then and saw them go will tell
you laughingly of their misfit outfits which bitterly-
won experience taught them so soon to cast aside
—stories the humour of which lies very close to
tears. There were many tragedies in those days;
and indeed if the tragedies to-day are fewer, they
are none the less terrible. Hunger and cold still
dog the heels of him who dares the pitiless North;
and Death waits ever by the trail.

But if life in the Farther North wears a grim
face, it is not always untouched with humour. The
pioneer has learned perforce the art of taking hardship gallantly. When the Provincial Legislature
met in 1909, the member from the Far North came
to Edmonton in a "caboose", and brought his family and his servant with him. The thermometer
stood at fifty below for a part of the time during
which their little house on runners was moving
slowly through the snow toward the Provincial
capital. It was a picnic under difficulties, but it
was a picnic still. And though the member and his
family lived in a hotel during the session, his wife
rose to the occasion by entertaining her friends at
afternoon tea in the "caboose". The M.L.A. and
his family went serenely back again by the same
conveyance when the session was over; and in the
following summer, fate intervened again to save
them from the commonplace; for the contest in
which the member sought re-election was delayed
two weeks, because the official counter from Edmonton found the rivers unnavigable on account of
ice, and had to walk the last one hundred and fifty
miles to the Riding.

These are some of the contrasts and some of the
elements that make life at the end of the line a spur
to the imagination and a healthful, heartening,
stirring thing. It is good to be here, and it is especially good to be here now. For, while the life of
this Far Northwest will never lose its zest and big-
ness, it will lose—as the indomitable industry of

man pushes the railroad beyond and ever beyond—
the unique charm that rests ever at the end of the
line.

*   *   *   *

This first impression, written in 1909, records, of
course, only a passing phase. Many of its details
are no longer true. The town, with the Canadian
National running through it to Vancouver, has long
since ceased to be the end of the line. Transcon-
tinentally, it has become what every railway station
was to me in my boyhood—a pausing-point on the
way to somewhere. But in another sense it has
become, not the end of the line, but, no less pictur-
esquely, the beginning. Tentacles of the railways
have reached northwestward to Peace River, and
due north to Fort McMurray, 305 miles from Edmonton. The Peace River country, practically *terra
incognita* in 1909, has become a great wheat-grow-
ing area. Some day, someone competent to do it
will write the story of the northward wheat-move-
ment—from the time when it was assumed that
wheat could not be grown north of Minnesota, to
the time when a graduate of the University of
Alberta won, year after year, the World's Cham-
pionship for wheat grown in the Peace River
country.

But these railway tentacles reach only a little way
into the fringe of the farther north. What lies beyond makes Edmonton, as I see it, the real beginning of the line. For where the railway tentacle

stops, the outposts begin. During the first five hundred miles north of McMurray, you will pass Forts Fitzgerald, Smith, Resolution, and Hay River. Then a long leap, and you will find yourself in Arctic Red River, 1,354 miles north of McMurray; Aklavik, 1,462 north of McMurray; Herschel Island, 1,587 miles north of McMurray. In those multiplying miles of the Silent Places, Indians will have given place to Eskimos, and you will have reached the Arctic Sea. Mingling with the native population in each successive northward stopping-place will be a sprinkling of white people— "Mounties", trappers, fur-agents, Hudson's Bay Company factors, teachers, doctors, nurses, missionaries. Anglo-Saxon-wise, these white people, thinly scattered through infinite distances, have become an intimate family. What made them so are the aeroplane and the radio. And, by virtue of the fact that it has become the focal point for aeroplane and radio, Edmonton has become the father of this family.

How intimate this family relationship is, you have only to sit up any Saturday night till midnight, and tune in your radio, to discover. For then, Edmonton "talks to the North". And talk it is. A budget of the week's news, local and foreign; interludes of good old dance tunes, "dedicated" to Miss Mary This at Fort Resolution or Jim That at Aklavik. "This is for you, Miss Mary." "This is for you, Jim." And again: "Hello, Harry Lewis at Beaver Lodge. Hello? Hello? Stand by, Harry.

Here's your girl, Harry, right here by the mike, wants to speak to you. Now, Joan!" And shy, excited Joan murmurs incoherently. Commonplaces? Could any words in the recognizable voice be commonplace? For that moment, Joan and Harry have the whole North to themselves. And, interspersed, personal items. Little Sally Jones, from Fort Smith, whom an Edmonton aeroplane brought to an Edmonton hospital for an appendicitis operation, is "getting better". Yesterday, those anxious parents would have been *incommunicado*— dog-team—six months. To-day the air speaks. Distance is annihilated. Edmonton and its remote, thinly-sprinkled, Anglo-Saxon family co-exist.

By radio, a doctor in the far north consults with an Edmonton specialist on the treatment of a case, or, if an epidemic threatens, sends for anti-toxin. The aeroplane, with its ear to the radio, speeds north on a "mercy-errand"; or casually carries a ton of mining machinery to Great Bear Lake or a ton of coal to Aklavik; or brings Arctic white fox pelts down to Edmonton, to adorn milady's coat.

'Tis a strange world, my masters. We who have grown old in this Edge of Things which is Edmonton feel it perhaps a little more vividly than the younger generation who have unthinkingly grown up into it. I have said as little as possible about it, because this is only a casual postscript to an essay written long ago. But some day someone will write adequately of this. I think that he will have to be a poet. For this is an epic theme.

SMALL BEGINNINGS

ON A DAY in June, 1908, the president of a university not yet in being, in a province which I had never heard of, in a country which I had never visited, came to Harvard and offered me the professorship of English. The offer sounded like midsummer madness. I think that what I accepted was, not the position or the salary, but the man. There was something about him that made me feel that to whatever no-man's land he went, there—somehow—the kind of university I should like to have a hand in would get to be. When I came to Edmonton in September of that year, I found him ensconced in the attic of a small brick public-school building. There assembled the four of us who were to constitute the faculty—veritable *philosophes sous les toits*—and he, and we, and it, were for the nonce the University of Alberta.

The scholastic background was Cambridge, McGill, Toronto, Columbia, California and Harvard. The four attic philosophers "professed" Classics, Moderns, Mathematics and Applied Science, and English Literature.

The school system of the province had been organized under the old territorial government, and was already in existence when the province was created. Public school and high school were therefore measurably developed; but the fact that the whole population was only 300,000, of whom a considerable proportion were illiterate immigrants, and the further fact that the remoteness of the province from the more highly developed life of the east created a dearth of good school-teachers, made the beginning of a university extraordinarily difficult. It was necessary to have a genuine university standard of matriculation. It was also necessary to have students. Outside of the little faculty, there were virtually only two men in the whole province who did not think the establishment of a university in a province only three years old utterly premature; those were the Scotch-Canadian Premier of the Province, who had the faith and foresight to make the immediate establishment of a provincial university the cardinal principle of his creed; and the president of the university who had come here to do just that thing, and had the bit in his teeth. It is with no sense of shame that I confess that there were compromises in those days. The only wonder is that there were so few; and if some of the forty-five students who gathered on those attic benches had not been subjected to too rigid an entrance standard, certainly no efforts were spared to help them make up their deficiencies.

In an attic, then, with a president, a faculty of four, and a student-body of forty-five, the University of Alberta began its work. It was a curious little family. Of the faculty there was not a man but had grown up in a great academic tradition, grooved and fixed through generations of development, with a student-body which by virtue of its size had lived a life of its own, and a group of professors who likewise lived a life apart. But these forty-five students were of the west, western, and had no traditions. I remember a solemn faculty meeting into which a student burst—to ask what kind of fountain pen we should recommend! I tried to imagine Eliot of Harvard meeting that situation with his grave and frigid courtesy! . . . .

In such an environment as this, and in a province where the few who bothered to think about the university at all, thought it premature, the university began to build. Not structures of brick or stone—that was not to come for several years—but the even more necessary structure of public sentiment. It would be hard, I fancy, for a student or member of the faculty of any old university to imagine what a university would be without its alumni—that great organized body of devotees, who respond to so many appeals and wield so much power, direct and indirect. We had no alumni and in the nature of the case should not have for a number of years. But scattered through the province, in numbers far larger than the casual observer would have suspected, were educated men and women, graduates of McGill and Toronto, of Dalhousie, of Oxford and Cambridge, of the Scotch universities and of universities in the middle west of the United States. If these were not alumni,

they could at least be made foster-sons; and so
"Convocation" was created, to which every man
or woman in the province with a college degree
could belong on the payment of a nominal fee.
Convocation elected representatives to the "University Senate" for a term of years; and these, with
the president and representatives similarly elected
from the university faculty, constituted the
academic governing body, responsible for the educational policy. Finances, on the other hand, were
placed under the control of the Board of Governors,
appointed by the "Lieutenant-Governor in Council"—that is to say, the political party in power.

Meanwhile, the president and faculty (we had
by now moved into somewhat more commodious
but still temporary quarters, and the life *sous les
toits* was only a memory) began the task of getting
into touch with these scattered three hundred thousand, and persuading them that there really was
a university in their province. Oh, those days of
"extension lectures!" What a nightmare, and at
the same time what a revelation they were! We
had to keep our regular work going and do justice
to it, and we had to travel by vehicle or some little
spur-line of the railway to every little rabbit-path
of a settlement in the province. The railway connections were well-nigh impossible; the hotels were
beyond the powers of a chaste vocabulary to describe. Sometimes we went to Calgary, the only
other sizeable city of the province; but the citizens
of Calgary wanted a university of their own, and

received us with mixed feelings. Sometimes we went down into the extreme southern part of the province—the Mormon country, where the disciples of Joseph Smith had established a thriving colony. Sometimes we followed the drift of settlement northward, where warily it was beginning to penetrate the edge of the Silent Places.

It was somewhere in the southern part, I remember, that my own extension lecture orbit reached its apogee. It was a Saturday night. There was a dance at the Oddfellows' Hall, and it was the one night of the week when there was a moving-picture show. When I entered the school hall to give my lecture (Heaven knows what it was about! It may have been Browning, for aught I know!) I found an audience of three grim old maids and four wriggling little boys. They were there I knew, *faute de mieux;* the old maids had no partners to take them to the dance, and the boys didn't have the price of the moving-picture show. I have felt ever since that there was a great opportunity missed. Why did I stubbornly inflict my lecture on those victims? Why didn't I rise to the occasion, give the boys ten cents apiece and proffer my escort to the ladies? But our best thoughts in this world come too late.

But those extension lectures were not without their gratifications. The number of educated men and women (Scotch, many of them) scattered through the province, was surprisingly large. You could never tell, sparse and forbidding though the

little settlement might be, what you would en-
counter there.   It was not unusual to have some
shaggy farmer rise after the lecture, and bur-r-r a
question at you which got to the very heart of your
little business, and meant no end of reading and
thought on the part of the questioner. And those
little post-lecture discussions, in uncouth surround-
ings, and under the light of smoky and sputtering
lamps, are among our pleasantest memories.

Those days are passed now. The extension work
has a staff of its own, more efficient because better
organized and because it has learned many lessons
of adaptation which we spasmodic lecturers of the
old *régime* could not readily understand. Places
which we struggled with recalcitrant train-sched-
ules and livery-stable "rigs" to get to, it speeds to
in motor cars, with boxes of picture-slides and all
the requisite machinery for extending and diluting
knowledge. Travelling libraries set out from the
university on their way to remote corners of the
province; and some years ago, Bishop Lucas, whose
diocese extended from Fort Simpson (twelve hundred miles north of Edmonton) northward to—oh,
well, say the north pole and be done with it!—
started back "home" again with an extension
library box of books among his supplies.

But I am anticipating. We should still be back
in the days when the path was yet untrodden and
policies just in the making. At least two of these
policies are worth recording here. It will be remembered that when the province came into being,

it was one of two which together filled in the gap between Manitoba and the Rockies. In both these provinces universities were created at about the same time; and because both were prairie provinces, depending upon essentially the same economic conditions, it might have been expected that their university development would have been on parallel lines. But instead a curious paradox developed. The president of the University of Saskatchewan, who had been a professor of Philosophy at Dalhousie, made it his first concern to establish agriculture on the curriculum, on the principle that if the obvious thing were done first, all things would be added unto him. The president of the University of Alberta, who had been a scientist at McGill, made it his first concern to establish and to foster the Arts curriculum, on the principle that if he did first the thing that was hardest to do in a purely agricultural community, the obvious things would come of themselves. Thus did *litterae humaniores* generate agriculture, and science become the father of the arts.

The second matter is interesting because it reflects the composite nature of university development in the Canadian West. By and large, the University of Alberta (and the same applies to the other western Canadian institutions) was modelled on the American universities. I believe that I am being indiscreet; for it has been the custom among Canadian university men to sneer at university-teaching in the States. This attitude has been a dissemination from Toronto—from which, of course, all righteous judgments come. But, however uncomfortably, it must be admitted that the University of Alberta, during those early years, developed along American lines. Whence it was that we piously gave "courses" of three "lectures" a week; required the students to attend them; watched the students taking notes of our pontifical utterances; got back a juvenile version on the final examination paper; saw to it that the examination paper contained evidence that they had read what we had told them to read; and counted the success- ful result as a "unit" toward the degree. With a small staff, and a student-body annually quad- rupling, it seemed to be about all that we could do. For that matter (1935) we do it yet, though com- pulsory attendance upon these formal "lectures" for third- and fourth-year students, has, happily, long since gone by the board, and "units" are dis- carded. But interpenetrating this Americanized machinery was another influence. We were a uni- versity within the British Empire. Pioneers and beginners though we were, we had inherited a tradition. That tradition, as I look back on it, seems to me to have been more Scottish than Eng- lish. We wanted from the outset to develop "pass- courses" and "honours-courses." The "pass-man" at Oxford doesn't need to take his work very seri- ously. The Public Schools have taught him man- ners (within his class), some facility in the classics, and a passable English style. He is already "finished". What he gets at Oxford is a grand good time, and a pass-degree. But we had no "gentlemen" to educate. Most of our students had had their preliminary training in the school of hard knocks. A few of them deserved—and got—the highly specialized training of an honours-course. But what most of them needed was the general training of the pass-course. Our desire, to the limit of our capacity (and I think we've kept that banner flying ever since), was to make that pass-course thorough, and never let it lapse into the casualness, the tolerant good-natured indifference, of the Oxford system. That is why I say that our tradition was more Scottish than English. What with the poverty of our students, their struggles to get an education (boys sweating in midsummer harvest-fields, gently nurtured girls going out to teach among uncouth immigrants)—and, incidentally, the fact that most of our best students were of Scottish descent—what with all this, our university in those early days seems to me a little Edinburgh rather than a little Oxford.

And with what zeal, what dour earnestness, those early students "went after" an education! Things are different now. About fifty per cent. of the students now, I should say, come to the university to get a grand good time—and get little else. But most of those early students wanted, not to cultivate their manners on the dancing floor, but to get an education in the traditional sense of the word.

We tried to give it to them. It was a strenuous job. We had little time to read and meditate in those days. When we weren't lecturing or "extensioning", we were answering the questions of those earnest students. Sometimes they were intelligent questions. Sometimes they were intended merely to impress the instructor with the student's interest in the subject (If young people could but realize how palpable such manoeuvrings are!). Sometimes they reflected the pathetic hope of a puzzled brain that "teacher" could give them some kind of nostrum, some magic prescription, which would enable them to pass the course. When you dryly said that the only thing you could recommend was hard study, their eyes dimmed with disappointment. "Is *this* all you can do for us?" their manner said, as they bowed themselves out of your office. But question us they did, in season and out of season. We were, you see, such a little family. It was natural then. But oddly enough, though twenty-some years have passed since those early times, and the university has become much larger and much more diversified, that early habit has not abated. As student and instructor, I had known several universities before I came to Alberta. The professors were as remote as gods on Olympus. The spectacle of a confident undergraduate barging in to the office of Kittredge of Harvard to ask him for a nostrum which would get the student through Kittredge's devastating Shakespeare-course simply transcends the imagination! But at the University of Alberta there was not then, and there is not yet, anything Olympian about us. Then, and still, the students of the University of Alberta assumed and assume that our time is theirs.

It is sometimes a little trying—but perhaps they are right.

LITTLE BROWN HOUSE

THERE is nothing distinctive about it. If you were bowling past it on the winding river-driveway you would get a fleeting impression of a bungalow, with brown shingled roof and brown shingled walls, with open porches two-thirds surrounding it. In winter you would see, through a tracery of bare branches, Little Brown House lifting from a smooth expanse of glistening snow. In summer, you would apprehend it as mere bits of brown wall and white wood-work, bowered in foliage of blue spruce and birch and Russian poplar and Manitoba maple, with honeysuckle bushes half concealing the porches. In front, on the other side of the driveway, you would see a wooded slope, dropping sharply down to the river bed of the Saskatchewan, with the valley, visible for miles in the clear air, marking out a great V, above the point of which you stand.

For two expatriates from a warmer climate, Little Brown House was the fruition of lessons learned in a hard school. Edmonton was a century old as a Hudson's Bay post when we came to it, but as a city it was in the mushroom stage. Houses were built with careless haste, and a perfect genius for producing pretentious "effects" with cheap materials. Our first two winters in a rented house

31

were a medley of chronically frozen pipes and rooms too arctic to be usable for six months of the year. We joked about it—but also we swore an oath that some day we should be warm in latitude 54, though we lived in a stoke-hole to accomplish it.

And then, one day, we happened to wander to the point of the V overlooking the Saskatchewan—and here forthwith Little Brown House cried unto us to give it being. The city had not reached out even a tentacle to it then. From the brow of the steep wooded valley, the untrodden snow stretched back to a low swell, on the crest of which was a little log cabin, with a log barn beside it. The father of the farmer who lived there had homesteaded it thirty years before, when the nearest railway station was Winnipeg, a trifle over eight hundred miles away. From the pioneer's son, himself no mean adventurer in the wild, we bought a little plot of ground, and then besought, from all and sundry, advice on the vital topic of how to keep warm at "forty below". Our own knowledge of building specifications was limited to a memory, albeit vague, of one who had built an ark of gopher-wood, had made rooms in it, had set a door in the side thereof, and had pitched it within and without with pitch. Gophers we had in abundance, but no gopher-wood. We thought we should need rooms, and perhaps also a window "in a cubit finished above". But of one thing we were sure—pitched within and without with pitch it must be—or whatever might be the equivalent in a sub-arctic climate. Building-

paper, then, of thickest hair-felt, clothed our
wooden frame, as with a perennial coat of fur.
Within, every room abutted upon a central chimney
of many flues, so that the radiation from the bricks
should supplement the piped warmth of the furnace.
The chimney, I remember, was built before even
the foundations were raised, and was completed
even to the brick-arched fire-places. There, for
many days, it remained, baring its domestic hearth-
stones to the middle air, till the slow carpenters
came to lift the structure round it, to swathe the
frame in that quintessential fur coat, and to apply
the epidermis of shingles. And, the next winter,
through double windows almost opaque with frost,
we peered out, content and warm, upon a frozen
world.

"Forty below!" It seems to be a sort of shib-
boleth among those who dwell south of the International Boundary, for the terrors of a northern
winter. "What do you wear?" "How can you
live?" "What can you do?"—asks the casual in-
quirer. But after all, when you have learned how
to deal with it, forty below (I have seen it sixty,
but fifteen or twenty degrees more or less after you
get that far don't really matter, and forty will do
for a standard)—after all, forty below is not a
terrible thing. It spells beauty, a beauty austere
and magnificent.

With us, the winter comes early. About August
twenty-fifth, there will probably be a touch of frost.
As we slip into September, the days remain hot—

intensely hot sometimes—but the nights grow
steadily colder, and frosts become a commonplace.
As September draws to a close the leaves either
gradually drop from the trees, or (more often) are
suddenly bitten off over night, by a severer frost,
and you wake up next morning to find only

"Bare ruin'd choirs, where late the sweet birds
    sang."

By October, the fields are sere, the trees have shed
all their shrivelled leaves, wild geese honk overhead
on their long southward journey, and the ground
begins to harden with a premonition of that iron
frozenness which will reach five feet beneath the
surface by mid-winter. The first snow-fall will
have come by now; and unless some exceptional
mid-winter thaw should occur, you may count on
having every dry hard little flake that falls to the
ground as your companion until the spring. Harder
and more deeply hard grows the ground as November passes, and between the fifteenth and the thir-
tieth of this month the river, that had rolled its
muddy torrent down one long arm of the V toward
Little Brown House and had bent sharply back
to its recession along the other arm, solidifies into
apparently indestructible ice. Soon the steel-blue
of the ice gives place to the white glitter of snow,
and the broad sinuous ribbon of the river becomes
a highway. With the advent of December, Winter
hesitates and seems almost to relent. The days

are at their shortest, with the sun rising at nine and setting at four, but there is a brief space of warmer weather. The dry, hard snow softens a little, and sometimes even indulges in a tentative thaw; you revel in the untrammelled freedom of temperate days. And then come January and February (twin monarchs of the frost) and with them—forty below!

Even then it is not persistent. I have seen it fluctuate around that temperature for six weeks at a stretch; but ordinarily it will come in short sharp attacks, with restful softenings between. A premonitory snow-fall—and then during the ensuing night the timbers of Little Brown House will begin to sigh and groan, as if some invisible hand were pushing and readjusting the beams. You do not need to look at the thermometer outside to know what is going on. The temperature is dropping, dropping. Next morning, you will look out upon a world, sunlit, frozen, silent. You will go out into it, of course. No one would wish to be immured from that dry, sharp, tonic air. If you are a novice, you will clothe yourself in a heavy fur coat. If you have learned of experience, you will substitute for the fur coat a lighter woollen garment. You will see to it that a fur cap comes well down over your ears, and that you are shod either with moccasins or with loose shoes of soft felt. As you tread upon the wooden side-walk, it cracks like a pistol-shot. You meet another pedestrian, and perhaps, though you may not be ten minutes from home, he

will stop you and tell you that your nose is frozen.
You rub it sharply with snow, and go on your way
rejoicing. You have been initiated into "forty
below". As you progress from the suburbs into
the city streets, you find yourself scanning every
passing nose with humorous intentness. Ah, there
is the tell-tale white spot at last. You halt him and
fraternally repay your debt. Teams strain past,
hauling heavy loads of coal. Sweat has frozen on
the horses; they are white from head to tail. Meanwhile, from every chimney, smoke rises, columnar,
unwavering, into the windless air. You are lured
back into the open spaces where the white quiet is.
Down in the valley, across the river, men are cut-
ting the dead wood and stunted poplars to open a
street, and at intervals of a hundred yards have
piled their cuttings and lighted them. The axe-
strokes are too far away to be audible. Out of the
silence the smoke-columns tower toward the sky,
regular as a company in open marching order,—
the giant body-guard of King Winter, watching over
a subjugated world.

And then, mayhap, when night falls, the Aurora
will come. Dim narrow spindrifts of light, with
blurred edges, stretch across the sky. Impercept-
ibly they gather and gather, a streamer here, a patch
of light there, from the whole northern sphere, making toward the zenith. The scattered streams and
zones converge, combine, and long slender arrows
of sharper light strike through them, radiating like
the spokes of a wheel from zenith to horizon, and

turning the arch of heaven into a gigantic cone, whose tapering point seems to have attained an infinite remoteness. And this point, this zenith, becomes suddenly a glory of living light. Masses of pink and green dissolve, resolve, blend, are flung like shimmering veils far down the horizon, and vanish only to reappear with added glory at the zenith. There is no rest to this mad dance of colour. Now it is flung out in nebulous masses, now shot forth in needle-like rays. Slowly the glory fades. The masses at the zenith break into luminous wisps, drift horizon-ward and disappear. And two expatriates, who have braved forty below to stand out in the open and watch the hour's pageant, slip back into the cheerful warmth of Little Brown House once more, while one quotes:

"What, you are stepping westward? Yea,
'Twould be a wildish destiny,
If we, who thus together roam,
In a strange land and far from home,
Were in this place the guests of chance:
Yet who would stop or fear to advance,
Though home or shelter he had none,
With such a sky to lead him on."

CAR NO. 1

CAR NO. 1 has gone now, whether to the junk-heap, or to a more punctilious career on some other part of the street-car line, I do not know; but the little neighbourhood group of us who daily watched its comings and goings will not soon forget that chapter of our annals in which it was the central figure; and to pay this tribute to its memory is a labour of love.

Picture to yourself a town of the Canadian Northwest—a town which dreamed that it was about to become a great city, and laid out its street-car system accordingly. The boom brought many remote sub-divisions into being. Out into these, among the "bush" and the prairie-chicken and the partridges, municipal ambition projected spur-lines, feelers, to serve the private ends of speculative aldermen, and to make glad the hearts of prospective suburbanites. At the end of such a spur we live, we and our half-a-dozen neighbours.

When our spur was finished, Car No. 1, which had already passed its brief heyday on the central lines, was relegated to us. Of an antique pattern, and somewhat battered, it seemed from the outset to adapt itself with a sigh of content to our quiet rusticity and casual schedule. The motorman and conductor who had served the system longest were rewarded with its care. The mile and a half which it had to "run" (one hesitates to use the word of a course so placid) was altogether immune from the risks and interruptions of the city streets. There were no "jams", vehicular or human, to block the way. Save for a wayward curve or two, the uncertainties of tracks laid without ballast upon a prairie soil, and the predilection of the trolley pole for jumping the wire and kicking riotously into space, Car No. 1 left its caretakers largely to their own leisurely devices.

It was this easy-going quality on the part of motorman and conductor, this informality fostered by distance from the crowded centres and immunity from official inspection, which created from the outset the *vie intime* of Car No. 1. It developed a sense of the amenities—not perhaps such amenities as pervaded the Back Bay horse car in the old Boston days when Oliver Wendell Holmes made of that antique vehicle an itinerant drawing-room— but amenities of a sort none the less. The motorman used to bring his wife and baby for a ride, and, during the long wait at the end of the line, was wont to walk up and down the aisle of the car, dandling his offspring and smiling proudly over its curly head at the waiting passenger. With a sterner but equally fatherly solicitude, he was known on more than one occasion to stop the car in mid-square, dismount, and spank the neighbourhood Bad Boy for risking his young life in front

of the moving fender. Not less concerned was he
for the safety of the wild life along the way. Many
a sudden grinding of the brakes as dusk approached
was due to the presence of a partridge or a cotton-
tail between the rails, dazed by the nearing head-
light. One day a wild duck led her brood out from
a pond beside which the line passed, and started
with them on an adventurous cross-country journey
to the river half a mile away. Near the end of the
line, where a curve blocked her way, she essayed to
cross the rails. The ducklings could manage pretty
well through the grass, but only a few of the largest
could scramble over the smooth little walls of steel.
With these the careless mother went on, leaving the
rest lamenting beside the obstruction. There the
motorman found them. The orphan family had
their one and only ride on a street car, back to the
pond. I like to fancy that in that quiet abiding
place, whence they had been so foolishly led and to
which so strangely restored, they grew to maturity
and escaped the hunter; and that they too have had
many a good chat with their feathered gossips, as
they winged southward over the international
boundary, about the amenities of Car No. 1.

The conductor was the presiding genius of Car
No. 1. With an elastic schedule, and on a spur-line
that was subject to municipal criticism for its lack
of patronage, it must needs be a very lethargic
seeker for a ride who could escape his watchful eye.
When the time approached for starting in from the
end of the line, he would hang far out from the

tail-board and survey the landscape with a lingering and hopeful look. Any distant moving object that might materialize into a human form was always given the benefit of the doubt. If one of our little neighbourhood group failed to appear at the wonted time, the conductor grew uneasy, and not infrequently allowed the scheduled minute to slip by unregarded. And if perchance, as he was in the act of pulling the bell-cord, a whistle or a shout came faintly to his ears, the wait was prolonged until the breathless late-comer could be pulled cheerily up on the high step. And when at last the car was speeding on its way, and the conductor spied a wanderer whose wave of hand, though it might be only by way of passing greeting, might also conceivably be a signal, the car came to a sort of interrogative pause. What mattered it if the wayfarer indifferently went on? 'Twas better to have loved and lost. And if some mother carrying a heavy child struggled toward us from a side-street, the conductor deserted the car altogether, and met her half-way to relieve her of her burden.

But this solicitude for the casual passenger was nothing in comparison with the intimate interest which he displayed in the little neighbourhood group of us who lived at the end of the line. Had we a letter to mail, he carried it in for us. As we were too far out to have the morning paper delivered, he purveyed the morning news. When our road was muddy, we wore overshoes as far as the car and consigned them to his care against our return. Did the clouds threaten, he would harbour our provident umbrella. If one member of the family were on the way home, and the other member of the family had but recently taken the car into town, the conductor would volunteer the most meticulous information. "Mr. Blank, your wife is not at home. She went in at half-past three. She did not carry her umbrella and I am afraid it is going to rain. And I don't think she had on overshoes."

But it was in the last run out from town at night that our conductor rose to sublime heights. It was at the utterly irrational hour of half-past ten that this last trip started—too early for the theatres, and too late to connect with the incoming or outgoing night railway trains. We called it the "Prayer-meetin' Special", because that was the only thing it could conceivably be for. But our inestimable conductor sustained a human relation to that most inhuman schedule. We *had*, you see, to make that car or walk; and when we would go in on the seven-thirty or the eight-thirty, he would invariably inquire of us whether we intended to catch the last car. If we answered in the affirmative, but did not arrive on time, he would wait as long as he dared, or as long as his diplomacy could keep the other passengers in a good humour. It was on such an occasion, that one of us whose tardiness had prolonged the wait a full fifteen minutes, overheard a crusty passenger mutter to the conductor: "Well, she's here. I guess you can start now, can't you?"

But alas! That schedule, with all its beautiful adaptiveness, contained within itself the germ of mortality. It is upon the schedule that I see the blame must fall, as I realize that I am recording a closed chapter of our annals. Time was when Car No. 1 ran undisturbed on its half-hour time-table, "the world forgetting, by the world forgot." It would reach the end of the line a long while before it was due to start back. It would drowse there, in the midst of woodsy silences, and little wild things would peer out of the bushes at it, and grow unafraid. If perchance the kindness of the conductor had delayed its course, that did but shorten its stay at the end of the line, and the half-hour schedule went placidly on. But the finances of the young city became a problem, and the municipally-owned street-car system ceased to pay. The city fathers were vexed, and looked askance at Car No. 1, with its few happy but unprofitable passengers. An expert—Oh, these modern efficiency experts that leave nothing undisturbed!—an expert took charge. The quiet little branch line was deprived of its integrity and woven into the system. Car No. 1 disappeared, and now a wretched modern thing, with an impersonal motorman and an austere conductor, is switched on to our branch, runs hastily out to the terminus, and dashes impatiently back again. Where Car No. 1 has gone, I do not know. I hope for its own sake that it has gone to its last resting place. But if it is condemned, as I fear it may be, to an active struggle with the harsh world, I know that its days are filled with regretful longing for those placid and kindly half-hour journeys, and the periods of quiet drowsing at the end of the line.

*   *   *   *

From the vantage-point of 1935, this sketch leaves the story half told. The boom passed. Depression came. Efficiency-experts vanished. The spur-line resumed its private life. Car No. 1, alas, did not come back. I suppose that it had been gathered to its fathers. But its successor has become, not merely an informal and companionable conveyance, but a club on wheels. The presiding genius (whose service as motor-man always seems quite incidental) is an elderly Scotchman, who was long ago a lighthouse keeper on his native shore, and who knew Robert Louis Stevenson and R. L. S.'s lighthouse father. The few bookish people at the end of the line are the club-members. The function of the motorman is to discuss Bobbie Burns and Tammas Carlyle with its members; to draw from his capacious pocket a quaint old edition of one or the other—or, for variety's sake, any other sound Scotch man of letters—and to see that the member reads it *en route*. But the period of transit is brief. The half-hour schedule affords a wide margin. Conversation is the thing. When the sojourn at the end of the line has been stretched to the last possible moment, the motor-man turns on the power, hurtles to the city junction more furious-

ly than did ever Jehu the son of Nimshi, speeds his
bounding rocking vehicle back to our suburban terminus, and recaptures his soul once more in the
contemplation of the Scotchmen whom he loves.

AT THE END OF THE LINE IN WAR TIME
(1916)

IF YOU will open your map of Canada and turn
to the province of Alberta, you will find in about
the centre of the province the town of Edmonton.
South of this point your map will be filled with the
names of other towns and villages and of a network
of railway lines—the ordered *minutiæ* of human
occupation. North of it you will find, in the main,
only magnificent and nameless distances—the
large silences of the map-maker. Your map will
trace for you a branch line of the Canadian Pacific
Railway which comes north to Edmonton and stops
here; and if it is unexpectedly up to date it will
contain a transcontinental which passes through
on its westward way; but for those who see that the
westward march of the pioneer is over and that
only northward new things await him, Edmonton
remains the end of the line.

Now turn to the side of your map and reckon
the parallel of latitude. You will figure it at about
54°. At any other time this parallel would interest
you only as it spelled certain climatic and indus-
trial conditions. It would suggest to you cold
winters, with nights that endure from four o'clock
in the afternoon to eight or nine in the morning,
and brief intense summers with an amazing fecund-

ity and rapidity of growth. It would mean for you
a wheat-grower's world south of us and around us;
and north of us a trapper's and a hunter's world—
a world of strange tracks in the snow, of moose and
elk and caribou moving warily through the Silent
Places. That is what latitude 54 would mean to
you at other times; but if you would know what it
means to us symbolically just now, you must take
a larger map, a map of both hemispheres. You
must trace that parallel around to the other side
of the world, and your moving finger will touch
Scarborough and go on through to the fleet-locked
harbour of Kiel. Conceive that imaginary line now
as a sensitive nerve along which thrills a feeling
and a passion, and you will be ready for the picture
I wish to draw for you—the picture of a town at
the edge of the Silent Places—a town inconceiv-
ably remote from the focus of the world's thought,
and yet vividly and grievously conscious that it too
is a part of the Empire at war.

Yesterday the local papers contained the head-
lines: "Last Bag of Mail for the Far North left City
this Morning." A few years ago that sack of mail
would have started behind a dog-team. Now the
sack will make the first lap of its journey by rail—
a short lap on an *antenna* of the transcontinental;
and where that *antenna* ends, the dog-team will
relay the sack to Fort Chipewyan, and other dog-
team relays will carry it by successive stages
through the rest of the seventeen hundred miles to

Fort McPherson. That will be a two months' journey; and here and there on that long route men are waiting, with a hunger which you whose ears are assailed with hourly cries of "Extra" cannot understand, for news of the war. Anywhere from three to six months after August, 1914, men drifted in from the north to learn for the first time that there *was* a war, and buried themselves for days thereafter in the files of the local dailies in a dazed effort to "catch up."

Can you conceive just what that would mean? Imagine yourself back, let us say, in December, 1914; and instead of having been able to assimilate the news, item by item, day by day, imagine yourself being compelled, all at once, to grasp the whole stunning mass of it! Bear in mind too as a part of the background of the picture that on these railway lines that stretch eastward from Edmonton over the prairies and westward from Edmonton toward the mountains, there are many little settlements, visible to the eye of the railway traveller only as a passenger station, a grain elevator, and a shop or two, but actually extending back for miles over scattered quarter-sections. To these little stations men will ride a far journey, and crowd the platform when the train is due. And as you stand on the rear platform looking back at the receding station, the little group will seem transfixed there, motionless save for the flutter of the unfolding newspapers. They have business, doubtless; they must get back to their farms; but for the moment there is nothing to be seen but that eager thrust for the news—the news from the front.

True, it is not a picture of the hinterland, the Silent Places, or even of the remote prairie or mountain railway station which I wish to draw for you. Edmonton is a town of perhaps fifty thousand inhabitants, and it has its two daily newspapers. But you cannot really see the picture of the town itself as an integral part of the Empire at war, unless you see it as a focal point, with the sparsely settled, news-hungry prairie around it, and the more sparsely settled, news-hungry Silent Places stretching indefinitely north of it—and from the prairie and from the Silent Places, men coming in by ones and twos and threes, with their traps left to rust on wilderness trails, or their reapers left to rust on hard-won acres—men hungry to know and hungry to go.

For, sophisticated as it is getting to be in spots, this Canadian Northwest is still a pioneer's world, a man's world. Native Canadians who had "come out" from eastern Canada and were "baching" in lonely quarters; Englishmen of birth and means who had established themselves on ranches; cockneys who had escaped from the overwhelming submersion of London poverty; Boer war veterans; men who had had professional military training but had not seen actual service—slowly but surely the call made its way out to them all, and slowly but surely they came in. When the war began, the population of the province of Alberta, which has an area about four times as large as all the New England States put together, numbered approximately 517,000. Of these, at the time of writing,* 18,000 have enlisted and are either at the front or being prepared to go. This is practically one fighting man out of every thirty men, women, and children. To accomplish this, there has been no conscription, nothing remotely resembling coercion, nothing more than the fine suasion of the call. In an older community, with the call coming from a "mother country" which many of them had never seen, this proportion of voluntary enlistments would be almost beyond belief. But this is a population of greater detachment, of fewer ties, less rooted to the soil,—and the apparently impossible is already the accomplished fact. And the end is not yet; for, as I write, comes the news of two more regiments to be recruited in the Edmonton district; and a prophecy from the D.C.O. that approximately 25,000 will enlist from the province before the war is over.

Yes, as far as the outlying districts are concerned, it is a detached population; and there, perhaps, there is not the same sense of desperate uprooting that there would be in an older community; but when you turn from the outlying districts to the town itself, the feeling is a pretty desperate one.

*December, 1915.

One in thirty! Aside from the larger philosophical sense in which the liberty of every fireside is involved, it means, in the vivid Western phrase, that everyone "has a stake" in the great enterprise.

At first, perhaps, this personal "stake" was not so vividly felt. The war seemed a grand game, a splendid triumphant thing that would be over in three or four months. The Fair grounds, with the long rows of horse- and cattle-sheds and the big exhibition pavilion became a barracks. Everywhere in the streets squads were drilling. On the campus of the Provincial University drill took the place of gymnasium exercise and athletic contests. On the suburban meadows, which we remembered as the farm lands of a few years ago, and the more recent battleground of real-estate speculators, cavalry deployed. The street-cars were filled with khaki, new faces mostly, men who had "come in". From Edmonton and the outlying districts, picked men, veterans, went to join the "Princess Pats", the pride of Canada. *They* went to the front, with the tragedy which nobody dreamed of already hanging over their heads; but of the many who were already enlisting, few seemed really *away*. Most of them were in local barracks, or at the Sarcee reserve in the southern part of the province, or, at the worst, at Valcartier. Nobody whom one knew seemed really to have crossed the Rubicon. Were they not still in Canada, with letters only a matter of a few days, and with a *known* address? The days when all the world would be "somewhere in France" were not yet.

Then came the news of what had happened to the "Princess Pats". You could not call it a casualty list. It was not even decimation. It was —annihilation. On a certain day in May, after having been reduced by what one may call normal casualties, they went into a charge 650 strong. They came out of it with only 175 living men. With that ended for us the first phase of the war— the phase when it was still only a grand game. But even yet it did not quite come home to us. The first contingent had consisted largely of men who had already seen service as privates in the British army, men of worth, but not of education. The second contingent—well, it is not safe to generalize, and there were many exceptions—but on the whole, so far as local impressions went, the second contingent seemed to consist chiefly of men who were out of a job and whose patriotic instincts were supplemented by the certainty of a berth. But the third contingent—that was a different matter. There went the cream of us—the University students, the little band of alumni accumulated through the brief years since the University was established, the young business and professional men—all the thoughtful young men who had said within themselves,—

"I do not know
Why yet I live to say, 'This thing's to do,'
Sith I have cause and will and strength and
          means
To do 't,—"

and who, no longer thinking too precisely on the
event, dedicated themselves forthwith to the cause.
From this time on the glamour ceased. Silently
the troopships slipped away, and one knew that
they had started only when news came of their safe
arrival. Valcartier was merely on the other side
of Canada. We could visualize it. But the vast
intricate organism of Salisbury Plain and Shorn-
cliffe, which was absorbing countless thousands
from all the world-wide supply-sources of the Empire—what could one make of that, here in this
remote town on the edge of the Silent Places?
Strange tales came to us, of chaotic conditions, of
utter discomfort, of mud more bottomless than
Alberta roads in springtime, of forced marches so
strenuous that hundreds of men dropped in their
tracks, of troops standing so long at attention that
they fainted by scores. What was it all for, this
apparent penalization of the men who had given
themselves to their country? And rumours began
to be rife that this unit or that unit had at last gone
to the front. For a time we believed them—believed them one day, to have them contradicted the
next. But at last we learned that the only indubit-
able news from the front was in the casualty lists.

It is a sad paradox, this—that your only means of knowing where your friend in a certain regiment is, is to know where his comrade was. And to-morrow your friend's name may be there, and you will cease to trace that regiment and some other eager watcher will profit by the information. Yes, the casualty lists began to come in, and here and there a father put a black band around his coat-sleeve or a mother or a wife quietly garbed herself in mourning. One woman had three sons at the front. One is dead now "somewhere in France"; one is a prisoner in Germany; and one lies desperately ill in a foreign hospital. But why multiply examples? This is merely war with the glamour gone. Meanwhile, as

> "Thousands speed
> And post o'er land and ocean without rest,"

begins the service of those who stand and wait. Social gaieties, involving expenditure for pleasure's sake, are discontinued. "Pay" affairs, the profits of which are to go to one of the many funds, crop up on every hand. Knitting women are every-where. They knit at concerts, at receptions, at dances, at lectures. Not Madame Defarge herself was more persistent in her vengeful task than are these women in their labour of love. If one is fated to lecture occasionally in their presence, these knitting women are a sort of challenge. "There!" they seem to say, "I am not exactly throwing down a gauntlet, but at least I am taking up a sock. If you think that you have anything to say that would warrant me in taking my eyes from this sock and my thoughts from the one who is to wear it, you are welcome to make the attempt; but I cannot encourage you." As to the results of this unceasing activity, they transcend the powers of the imagination. If one woman in her leisure moments can knit one sock in two days and if something more than fifty per cent. of all the women who concern themselves about the war are thus engaged, how long will it take to knit enough socks to reach from Ypres to Berlin—but I am no mathematician! However, the letters that come from the trenches say that one pair of socks lasts only two days.

In any event, what really staggers the imagination is that these homely little things do actually find their way through the welter to the very one for whom they are intended. It is a curious thing, this intimacy between a fireside here in northwest Canada and a dugout or a trench somewhere in France. I sat at such a fireside the other day, and listened to a batch of letters from a dugout. The mother read them quietly, with only a little catch in her voice now and then. The boy—he is only eighteen—wrote, of course, of the usual things— the long toil in the trenches, the scream of the shells, an occasional aeroplane battle overhead, the danger (so lightly touched!), the loss of a comrade. But the real charm of the letters lay in the simple little details of his daily routine: how, as he put it, he "managed"; and it was this which brought the fireside and the dugout so close together. And then the mother, urged by these simple details, told how, each week, she sent a parcel: towels—there is a dearth of them at the front; half-worn suits of underclothing—with washing almost impossible, it was easier for him to wear a cheap suit and throw it away; handkerchiefs—his nose, he wrote her with boyish humour, was not recognized by the government. Into every parcel too went cookies and a bar of chocolate; and every little while a fruit-cake, warranted to mellow *en route*, started on its long journey to the dugout. The earlier letters, before these little extras began to arrive, were full of appeals for "sweets"; the later, full of gratitude for just these favours. There was a curious pathos about these letters—not in the language, for there was no snivelling in them; but unconsciously, in the picture which they evoked. Only eighteen, all boy yet, hailing the arrival of a pot of jam as an event; but somehow all man too, making light of the physical torture of the muddy trenches; glossing over the danger; ending every letter with an insistent "Now *please* don't worry, mother!" And that mother sitting there, not knowing just where the boy was, content perforce with the hope that he was still somewhere, and following him into the awful welter with all these homely little things! Was not this what she had been doing, this "looking out" for him, from his infancy? And she would keep on doing it—to the end.

Well, I suppose this tale of socks and underclothes and jam and chocolate is commonplace enough; but I confess that as I sat by the fireside and thought how many thousands of other firesides there were now just like that, I fell to wondering whether "the nations at war" were not paying almost too large a price for "discovering their souls". I saw under that mother's restraint of manner, the desperate fear, every time she sent the homely little parcel, that the boy might not be there to receive and enjoy it. There was evidence of such a good citizen and such a good true man in those simple-hearted, manly, and thoughtful letters; and one of the multitudinous fragments of a blind shrapnel might have put an end to him while we sat there.

After all, any human life, and particularly any young life full of the promise of fine things, is a big thing to waste in the casual way in which war wastes it. I think that those of you who live in great cities cannot realize that quite as vividly as we do. A city of anywhere from half a million to two or three million inhabitants is conceived on too great a scale. Half-a-dozen men and women lose their lives in a tenement-fire; you see their names in next morning's paper and in most cases neither their names nor the street they lived on means anything to you. Death has a way, for long years, of touching only the periphery of your experience.

But with us in a little town, death is somehow a more intimate thing. If you do not know the man himself, you are fairly certain to know a relative of his, or at least to have some knowledge of the little circle in which he moved. Life is small enough for one to *see* every man in his relation to the community. And so I wonder if perhaps you drift more readily than we into conceiving of those men who die daily in France or Russia or the Balkans merely as pawns in the great game. Am I wrong in thinking that we see them more in their relation to a fireside somewhere, and to a civic life in which they might have played a useful part? No, I am afraid I am no longer capable of commercing with the skies, as I think of the war. More and more it is getting to mean to me nothing but a tragedy of thwarted lives.

But for those of us who only stand and wait, it is not all grey. There are stories of the heroism of "our boys" that stir us beyond words—stories, too, that change with astonishing abruptness our estimates of those whom we had too lightly regarded. There was a certain youth, for example, for whom I fear that I had had scant respect during his student life: a sickly fellow with rather a hang-dog air. He was out of his classes a good deal of the time and he was not successful in examinations. I believe that I suspected him of malingering. He tried to enlist and was turned down by the medical inspector, and tried again and yet again without success. How he ever got in, nobody could understand; but one day he went, and we shook our heads and prophesied that he would be incapacitated in a week or two. We heard no more of him until word came in letters from his friends that he had quietly picked up a smoking bomb and thrown it clear of the trench before it exploded, and then had climbed out in the face of the flying bullets and brought in a wounded comrade. And this was he who had only last year seemed such a faint-hearted traveller along life's common way!

And, after many months, when the permanently invalided soldiers began to come back—how the local newspapers recorded every stage of their long railroad journey from Montreal westward! And how, when the train at last reached Edmonton, the mayor and the citizens and the regiments still in barracks crowded the platform to welcome them! Here was one who had been on the battle cruiser *Isis* in the Boxer Rebellion of 1900, had enlisted with the "Princess Pats", and had, as he cheerfully expressed it, "got his" at Ypres. And this "veteran" was hardly past his twenties! Here was another who had been shot in the nose, the bullet passing out at the back of his head. But he was "none the worse" and his wrath at not being permitted to return to the trenches was still simmering. Shattered arms, shrapnel wounds in thigh or back or shoulders— these were trifles. They would tell you how they got them if you insisted; but they really wanted to talk about the bravery of this officer or that comrade who alas! would have no other epitaph. It was only those who had been "gassed" who could not enjoy and reciprocate our enthusiasm. They, poor fellows, had to be shipped quietly away, and cared for in the hope that some day they would be themselves again.

Ypres, Festubert, Givenchy—how real they seem as we talk to these men who have been there! To have been there one's self in the closed chapter of leisurely travel before the war counts for nothing. The time has passed when names in Belgium and in northern France meant places. They mean deeds. They were static once. They are dynamic now. And you can see Ypres more vividly through a crude and incoherent narrative *plus* an empty sleeve than you can through all the skilful and well-ordered descriptions of the war correspondents. Curious how in this world-business one's geographical reach expands. We seem so far from everywhere, up here on the edge of the wilderness. We have to travel nearly a thousand miles to reach the nearest "metropolis", and Winnipeg is provincial enough! Two years ago we seemed utterly off by ourselves. Ypres, Festubert, Givenchy! Our family physician, who seemed preordained by nature to spend his days like a mouse in a hole, writes to us from Alexandria, where he is serving with a base hospital that receives the wounded from the Dardanelles; and to-morrow one's next door neighbour may be invalided home from Mesopotamia!

And how quaintly touched with humour, sometimes, are these sudden changes in perspective! There was a Dane who used to own a little brick-yard down by the river. It was a small business and we remember him as occasionally driving a load of bricks himself and delivering them at the University buildings. But he had seen service, and it was not long after the war began before he received his commission as major. In time he was captured by the Germans at Ypres, and interned in the little town of Bischofswerda one hundred miles south of Berlin, near the Austrian border. He could speak German perfectly—had learned it as a boy in Denmark—and he determined to attempt the impossible and escape. Hiding in a well in the internment camp just as the prisoners were about to be shut up for the night, he crept away at dusk, eluded the double guards, and turned his face, not toward the Austrian border whither they would naturally set out in pursuit, but toward Berlin. He made his way to a village, found a newspaper containing the statement that he had escaped and was making his way toward Switzerland, bought a raincoat to cover his uniform, and then started on his perilous journey. In Berlin, with delightful effrontery, he took a taxi-ride down the Unter-den-Linden. How Dumas would have revelled in the story! Then

this Danish d'Artagnan disguised himself as a
bricklayer and, after many adventures, including
a trip through the Kiel Canal, reached Denmark,
whence the British consul sent him to England.
And now he has been formally received by the King
at Buckingham Palace, and is detained at the War
Office to report on conditions in Germany. From
the little brickyard beside the Saskatchewan to
Ypres; from Ypres to Bischofswerda; from Bischofswerda to Berlin; from Berlin to Buckingham
Palace—"and so home", as Pepys would say, to
the brickyard. And two years ago we were entertaining d'Artagnan unawares! Well, there will be
no unawareness when he returns to spend the
Christmas holidays in Edmonton.

So it goes, here at the end of the line in war time
—grey days and bright ones, bitter bereavements
shared by a whole community, intense anxieties
which no philosophy can dispel, new elations as the
commonplace men of yesterday become the heroes
of to-day, passionate news-hunger in the Silent
Places, sparse districts becoming ever sparser as
the men come in and keep coming in, to share in
the great thing that is to do. I hope that you have
seen, as I seem to see, that there is a kind of unity
to it all—a unity that springs from our very remoteness from the great scene upon which all our
thoughts are fixed. But I cannot help thinking
that there is another meaning as well. These are
rather dark days just now in the great struggle—

days of halting, of uncertainty, of occasional defeat. But just as the men come in and keep coming in here, so do they come in and keep coming in in thousands of other remote little places all over the Empire. It is a slow process, but there isn't any limit to it. And nobody doubts what the end will be.

THE LONG ARM OF THE LAW

IN THE Canadian province of Alberta, before the Chief Justice of the Supreme Court of the province, two Coppermine Eskimos, Sinnisiak and Uluksuk, were tried for murder. Behind this brief record of the orderly processes of British justice lies a strange story.

If you will take down your map of the Arctic, you will find on the northern coast of the continent, in about lat. 68, long. 115, the point at which the Coppermine River flows into Coronation Gulf. From the time of the earliest records, that frozen bit of the earth's surface has borne a sinister reputation. In 1771, Samuel Hearne, the first white man to enter the region, stood by while his Indian escort massacred a settlement of Eskimos. Hearne named this spot (about five miles up from the mouth) Bloody Fall. Fifty years later Captain (afterwards Sir) John Franklin lost nearly all of his escort and several of his officers in the same region. In Captain Franklin's *Narrative of a Journey to the Shores of the Polar Sea*, there is a pen-and-ink sketch of Bloody Fall. In the foreground is depicted a pile of human skulls.

The Eskimos of this region, near kinsmen of the famous Blond Eskimos whom Stefansson discovered, are virtually a prehistoric race. Stefans-

son describes the Coppermine tribe as wholly untouched by civilization, dependent upon bow and
spear, ignorant of the use of fire-arms until he
visited them, ignorant even of the use of nets in
catching the fish upon which they depend largely
for food. Like the Blond Eskimo, "their existence
on the same continent with our populous cities is an
anachronism of ten thousand years in intelligence
and material development."

In the summer of 1913, two Roman Catholic
priests from the far northern mission of Fort Norman, Father Rouvière and Father Le Roux, determined to venture into the region around the mouth
of the Coppermine in order to Christianize this
tribe. For two years after their departure from
Fort Norman, nothing was heard from them or
about them. Then rumours began to come to the
ears of the members of the Royal Northwest
Mounted Police in the far north that Eskimos had
been seen wearing the cassocks of the missing
priests. These rumours were embodied in a report
to headquarters, and with the arrival of this report
the real story begins.

It was decided at once to send out a patrol of the
R.N.W.M.P. to ascertain the fate of the priests,
and if they had been murdered, to bring the murderers to justice. The long arm of the law made
ready to reach out over the frozen north. You may
conceive the shoulder of that arm as being at
Edmonton, capital of the Province of Alberta.
Edmonton, albeit more than two thousand miles

due south of the Coppermine region, is the court of nearest jurisdiction. Here, if there had been a murder, the murderers should be brought and tried.

The hazardous journey, much of it over barren Arctic lands almost unknown and only vaguely mapped, could not be made in less than two years. The men appointed to make it would have to cut themselves loose from civilization and from any sort of communication with headquarters. Among a probably hostile people whose speech they could not understand, they would have to ascertain the fate of the priests, and, if the priests had been murdered, gather such evidence against the murderers as would pass muster in a British court; they would have to find the murderers, and arrest them; and they would have to bring them back.

The leadership of this patrol was intrusted to C. D. La Nauze, a youth of twenty-five. La Nauze was born in Ireland of French-Huguenot ancestry. His father had also been in the Mounted Police in the Edmonton district, but had gone back to Ireland on inheriting a small property. La Nauze was a constable, or, in its military equivalent, a private, in the Police force. When he was selected for this mission, he was promoted to an Inspectorship, a rare honour for so young a man. Neither he nor the two constables selected to accompany him knew a word of Eskimo speech or had ever been to the far north. But after all, that didn't matter. He had his orders to get the evidence and get the men— and he went.

Inspector La Nauze and his companions outfitted in Edmonton in May, 1915, with equipment and supplies for two years. A railway trip of three hundred miles brought them past the Arctic Divide to Peace River Landing. From there the H.B.C. transport and the steamer *MacKenzie* carried them down the Peace River and the MacKenzie. At Fort Norman they could get no further news of the missing priests, nor could they secure an interpreter or guide. The Indians of Fort Norman were afraid to venture among the Eskimos. At Fort Mac-Pherson, however, 1,800 miles north of Edmonton, they found an Eskimo named Ilivanik, who had been four years with Stefansson and who is frequently mentioned in Stefansson's *My Life with the Eskimo*. Ilivanik refused to go without his wife and daughter, so the adaptable inspector added all three to the party, and set the woman making deer-skin clothing. Then the patrol returned to Fort Norman, where they met the explorer, D'Arcy Arden. From Arden and from an Indian boy who had accompanied him to Dease Bay the preceding summer, Inspector La Nauze obtained confirmation of the report that the priests' cabin at Dease Bay had been dismantled, and that Eskimos had been seen carrying their rifle and wearing their cassocks. Arden consented to accompany the party as guide, and Arden and Ilivanik were appointed special constables.

Thus constituted, the little party set out from Fort Norman, with a York boat, and two canoes.

Ninety miles up the swift Bear River they made
their way, "tracking" the heavily laden boats for
much of the distance, sometimes spending whole
days waist deep in the icy water; in one instance
taking four days to gain a single mile; and reaching
Great Bear Lake after forty-three days of hard
going. From the mouth of the Bear River they
sailed three hundred and fifty miles across the Lake,
often having to put in at shallow harbours to escape
the storms, and on more than one occasion paying
the inevitable penalty of landsmen who risk the
high seas. At last, on the 13th of September they
reached Dease Bay, which was to be their permanent base and from which they were to make their
start into the unknown.

After a brief rest, the little party set out by dog
train to the barren lands where the priests had gone
on their fatal mission. On the 28 of September "we
arrived", reports the inspector, "at the tiny cabin
we had come so far to find, and found everything
in ruins and not a sign or clue to show the where-
abouts of the missing priests." From here the patrol
returned to their base at Dease Bay. There they
wintered, and in March of 1916 set out for the
Coppermine.

On the first of May, 1916, they found themselves
among the Coppermine Eskimos. To the first
whom they encountered the inspector explained that
he and his companions "had been sent by the Big
White Chief to look after the people." Here they
were joined by Corporal Bruce, of the R.N.W.M.P.,

who had been travelling with a section of the Canadian Arctic Expedition, and had seen an Eskimo named Uluksuk wearing a cassock belonging to one of the missing priests.

A week later the patrol reached a large village of Eskimos among whom were two brothers, Nachin and Ekkeshuina, whom Ilivanik recognized as former acquaintances. What happened then can best be told in the inspector's own words:

"Ilivanik thought he could find out something from these people, so said we would go to their house, and we were escorted to a small snow hut in the middle of the village. I then asked them if they knew of any white man who had been to Imaerinik.* 'Oh, yes, they had met several.' I then sat back and let Ilivanik do the talking. I heard him question them closely and I could see him trembling. I saw that something was happening but I never moved, and in about five minutes he turned to me and said: 'I got him, the priests were killed by Husky (Eskimo) all right; these men very very sorry.' And indeed they appeared to be; they both had covered their faces with their hands, and there was a dead silence in the igloo.

"I told Ilivanik to go ahead while I went out for Corp. Bruce, and when we got back Ilivanik said, 'Now you write down these two names, Uluksuk and Sinnisiak, you got that? Now I find out some more.' Meanwhile several other Eskimos had entered the igloo, and while Ilivanik was talking to Ekkeshuina, an elderly man named Koeha was

*Lake Rouvière, southwest of Bloody Fall. Source of Dease River. Named after Father Rouvière who built a cabin there.

joining in the conversation in the usual Eskimo manner. Ilivanik ordered only one man to speak at once, and they said Koeha had better speak as he knew all.

"Without any hesitation Koeha gave a clear and concise account of the whole affair as he had heard it, and it was 4 a.m. when he had finished with his statement."

Koeha, it may be noted in passing, was subsequently brought down to Edmonton to bear witness at the trial.

On the strength of the information gained from Koeha, and supplemented by other members of the tribe, Corporal Bruce laid a formal charge before the inspector against Uluksuk and Sinnisiak. Learning that Sinnisiak was hunting on the ice somewhere near the coast of Victoria Land, the party proceeded to Bernard Harbour, the southern headquarters of the Canadian Arctic Expedition, and from there struck across the ice of Dolphin and Union Straits. After being once thwarted by the fog they succeeded in crossing the Straits, and near the coast of Victoria Land they found a skin village of Eskimos. Among the curious throng that gathered round the visitors one of the Eskimo guides recognized the wife of the man whom they were seeking. Leaving one of the constables in charge of the sleds, the inspector with the other constable, Corporal Bruce, and Ilivanik, followed the woman to Sinnisiak's tent. Sinnisiak was sitting and he did not rise. "What do you men

want?" he said. "The white men here want you
to go with them," replied Ilivanik. "If the white
men kill me," said Sinnisiak, "I will make medicine
and the ship will go down in the ice and all will
be drowned." By this time the tent was crowded
with spectators, but instead of resisting or attacking
the white men, they said to Sinnisiak, "Yes, you
must go with the white man and do what he tells
you." At length Sinnisiak rose trembling to his
feet. Just behind him were two hunting knives
and a .22 automatic rifle. Corporal Bruce then
formally arrested him, and he was led out without
further difficulty Meanwhile, search of other tents
in the vicinity had revealed a rifle answering in all
respects to the description of the one possessed by
Father Rouvière. This the inspector purchased,
and the party returned across the Straits to Bernard
Harbour.

Three days later, the inspector in his capacity of
justice of the peace (all members of the R.N.W.
M.P. are J.P.'s), held a preliminary hearing at
which Corporal Bruce and Ilivanik gave evidence
for the prosecution. The prisoner was warned
through the interpreter that he need not incriminate
himself. He replied, "I want to speak," and made
a confession of the crime. The murder, it appeared,
had occurred near Bloody Fall, place of tragic
memories. The priests, after an altercation with
one of the Eskimos, had left hurriedly with only a
few dogs. Sinnisiak and Uluksuk had followed

them, and when they had caught up with the priests
had been forced to aid the dogs in dragging the
sled. Making an excuse to throw off the harness,
Sinnisiak had slipped behind the sled and stabbed
Father Le Roux in the back. Father Rouvière had
attempted to escape. Sinnisiak, lifting the priest's
rifle from the sled, shot him as he ran, and Uluksuk
finished him with the knife.

On the strength of this confession and the cir-
cumstantial evidence, Inspector La Nauze formally
committed Sinnisiak for trial on two charges of
murder. Leaving the prisoner at Bernard Harbour in charge of Corporal Bruce, and adding to his
own party a youth of mixed Eskimo and Norwegian
blood named Patsy, who was destined later to play
a picturesque part at the trial, the inspector set out
to find Uluksuk. It was rumoured that Uluksuk
was hunting near the mouth of the Coppermine.
By great good luck the first group of Eskimos encountered there included the man whom they were
seeking. He was arrested without difficulty, his
deposition taken according to the usual routine,
and he was committed for trial on the same charges
as Sinnisiak.

Here the party broke up. The two constables
and Ilivanik set out for Great Bear Lake and Fort
Norman, intending to visit the scene of the murder
en route and collect whatever relics of the murdered men they could find. Inspector La Nauze
with Patsy and Uluksuk returned to Bernard Harbour, and thence, with Corporal Bruce and Sin-

nisiak, sailed on the *Alaska* (a steamship of the Canadian Arctic Expedition) to Herschell Island.

At Herschell Island, which is at the northern tip of the Yukon and just off the northeastern corner of Alaska, there is a regular station of the R.N.W. M.P. With the handing over of the prisoners to the constituted authorities, the immediate task of the patrol was finished. They had set out from Edmonton in May, 1915. From their first base on Great Bear Lake they had travelled 1,400 miles, much of it over practically unknown territory. It was now the 28th of July, 1916, and they were compelled to winter at Herschell Island.

The spring of 1917 brought them to the last chapter of the story. Up the MacKenzie and the Peace they came. The chug of the steamboat, the whistle of the train waiting at Peace River Landing to speed them to Edmonton sounded a welcome to the inspector from the world upon which he had turned his back two years before. But Sinnisiak and Uluksuk, Ilivanik and Patsy and Koeha— creatures of a prehistoric past, children of the Stone Age—what must they have thought, as this boat without oars, this sled without dogs, rushed them into the twentieth century?

They reached Edmonton on the 8th of August, and the trial, with the characteristic promptness of Canadian justice, followed hard upon their arrival. It was a strange scene which met the eye of those of us who sat as spectators in the court-room. The room itself, high ceilinged, toned to a dark oak panelling, measured perhaps thirty feet square. Upon the dais, behind the desk which amply fenced it off, sat the Chief Justice in his black robes. Underneath a crown of white hair, his face showed round, smooth, without a wrinkle, delicately flushed, a little remote—the face of a man who had spent his life in the serene contemplation of the law. At the long table directly beneath the dais sat the lawyers appointed by the Dominion Government at Ottawa respectively to prosecute and to defend these inarticulate wards of the Crown. The lawyers, too, were in their black robes, and before them on the table lay a strange *congeries* of objects —a .44 Winchester rifle much rusted from exposure, a blood-stained cassock, several breviaries, a surplice, an alb, a crucifix, a patina, an old yellow diary half weathered away; and gruesomely distinct, the lower jaw bone of a human being with the teeth intact. Beyond the far end of the table, with their backs to the side wall, sat the six jurors,*—solid, substantial and rather weather-beaten faces, among which one face stood out with startling distinctness, square-jawed, high cheek-boned, hawk-nosed, keen-eyed, bronzed, the face of an ex-manager of the H.B.C. district, who had spent his life in the north country. And, finally, in the oak-panelled prisoner's box, just behind the lawyers' table, and facing

---

*Alberta follows the tradition of the old Northwest Territories in having a jury of six instead of twelve.

the judge, sat Sinnisiak, the Coppermine Eskimo, on trial for his life.

The prosecution had elected to try the prisoners separately, and Sinnisiak sat alone. And how very much alone he looked! He was clad in caribou skins, and the sweat poured from him as he sat in the close hot room. The scant black beard on his chin and the close-cropped black hair accentuated the pallor of his erstwhile swarthy skin. His heavy bullet head, with its high cheek-bones, was tilted slightly forward. His narrow-set, protuberant eyes, with their small pupils and abnormally vivid whites, were fixed in a dull unblinking stare. What was he thinking of as he sat there, understanding no word of the lawyers' pleas and counterpleas? Mr. H. G. Wells in his *Time Machine* describes the experience of a man who succeeded in transporting himself thousands of years into the future, and watching for a little while the doings of generations yet unborn. No Time Machine of Sinnisiak's invention, but the long arm of a law of which he had never heard had snatched him from his tribe and brought him three thousand miles and ten thousand years into an unknown world. Nor was he a mere spectator. Somehow the world was focused upon him. Among his tribesmen were no courts of justice. An eye for an eye and a tooth for a tooth was all that he knew. If you killed a man, his relatives killed you if they were strong enough, submitted tamely if they were not. What did al!

this mean? From without, through the open windows came the rumble of street cars and the roar of motors. Within, the voices of the lawyers rose and fell, broken in upon occasionally by the low voice of the judge.

Of many of the details of the trial it is superfluous to write. They did not differ in form from any other trial. The prosecutor made his opening speech. Inspector La Nauze, tall, lithe, broadshouldered, blue-eyed, vividly handsome in his R.N.W.M.P. uniform, gave his testimony. The rifle, the diary, the garments and religious paraphernalia of the murdered priests, and the one gruesome human relic which had rewarded the search, were definitely or plausibly identified. And then old Koeha took the stand, with Ilivanik as interpreter. To Koeha, with Ilivanik's aid, the clerk sought to administer the oath. But of the wordy and intricate phraseology of the law, interpreter and witness could make nothing. For once the time-hallowed phrases had to give way to an oath such as no clerk in a British court of justice had ever administered before. "Speak straight now. Do not speak with two tongues," said the clerk to Ilivanik. "Speak straight now. Do not speak with two tongues." said Ilivanik to Koeha. And Koeha and Ilivanik kissed the Book.

Of Koeha's testimony, again, it is superfluous to tell. The procedure of the law is a thing of endless repetitions. Suffice it, that Ilivanik's mind seemed to have lost the pliancy which both Stefansson and

La Nauze had attributed to it. The poor fellow was sadly muddled by the complex sentences of those who, through him, sought to question the witness. Time after time the more experienced La Nauze had to intervene. "Can you identify this rifle?" asks the lawyer. Ilivanik stolidly shakes his head. "Whose rifle was this?" aids the judge. Again Ilivanik shakes his head. "Who belong rifle?" the inspector helps out. A gleam of intelligence appears on Ilivanik's face. He turns eagerly to Koeha. There is endless guttural monotone between them; and at last, Ilivanik is ready to translate Koeha's answer. But even with La Nauze's help things continue to go badly. The long conversations between Ilivanik and Koeha are wholly disproportionate to the meagre results. Ilivanik is even suspected of surreptitiously threatening the witness and "putting him through the third degree". Finally, Patsy is substituted for Ilivanik and at once a new personality is felt. A slight dark-eyed boy of seventeen, Patsy has a face which is almost aristocratic. He is alert and catches instantly what he is asked to transmit. In contrast to the fixed stolidity of his companions, Patsy's eyes dart everywhere and there is a gleam of mischief in them. His answers, promptly obtained from Koeha, and promptly and clearly rendered, have a humorous twist.

The struggle of refractory tongues ends. Corporal Bruce and the constables give their testimony; and then at last the dramatic moment comes

and Sinnisiak himself takes the stand. He takes
the oath to "speak straight, not to speak two
tongues", and kisses the Book. He is told that he
is under no compulsion to speak, and replies, "I
want to speak." And then, to the hushed court-
room with its twentieth century noises coming
through the windows and its twentieth century men
and women listening, and its black-robed, calmly
remote judge, and its eagerly intent jurors, this
man of the Stone Age tells his primitive elemental
story. Word for word he tells it as he told it to
Inspector La Nauze many months ago. There is
no imagination in him to vary the story. And
sentence by sentence, in tones low but wholly
audible in the hush, the interpreter translates:

"I was stopping at the mouth of the Coppermine
river and was going fishing one morning. A lot of
people were going fishing. When the sun had not
gone down I returned to camp and saw that the
two priests had started back up the river. They
had four dogs; I saw no other men.

"I slept one night. Next morning I started with
one dog to help people coming from the south. All
day I walked along and then I left the river and
travelled on land; I was following the priests' trail.
I met the priests near a lake; when I was close to
them, one man came to meet me.

"The man Ilogoak (Father LeRoux), the big
man, came to me and told me to come over to the
camp. Ilogoak said, 'If you help me pull the sled,
I will pay you in traps.' We moved off the same
day I arrived, to be near wood. Uluksuk was with

me and we pulled the sled. We could not make the trees; it was hard work, and we made camp.

"The next day we started back and the priests were going ahead; it started to storm and we lost the road. After that the dogs smelt something and Uluksuk went to see what it was, and I stayed behind. Uluksuk found that it was a cache of the priests and told me to come over. As soon as we came there the priests came back. Ilogoak was carrying a rifle; he was mad with us when we had started back from their camp. and I could not understand his talk.

"I asked Ilogoak if he was going to kill me, and he nodded his head.

"Ilogoak said, 'Come over to the sled,' and he pushed me with his hand.

"The priests wanted to start again, and he pushed me again and wanted me to put on the harness and then he took his rifle out on top of the sled. I was scared and I started to pull.

"We went a little way and Uluksuk and I started to talk and Ilogoak put his hand on my mouth. Ilogoak was very mad and was pushing me. I was thinking hard and crying and very scared and the frost was in my boots and I was cold. I wanted to go back, but I was afraid. Ilogoak would not let us. Every time the sled stuck, Ilogoak would pull out the rifle. I got hot inside my body, and every time Ilogoak pulled out the rifle I was very much afraid.

"I said to Uluksuk, 'I think they will kill us.' I can't get back now. I was thinking I will not see my people any more, I will try and kill him. I was pulling ahead of the dogs. We came to a small hill, I took off the harness quick and ran to one side and Ilogoak ran after me and pushed me back to the sled. I took off my belt and told Ilogoak I was going to relieve myself, as I did not want to go to the sled. After that I ran behind the sled, I did not want to relieve myself. Then Ilogoak turned round and saw me; he looked away from me and I stabbed him in the back with a knife. I then told Uluksuk, 'You take the rifle.' Ilogoak ran ahead of the sled and Uluksuk went after him. The other white man wanted to come back to the sled; I had the knife in my hand and he went away again.

"Uluksuk and Ilogoak were wrestling for the rifle, and after that Uluksuk finished up Ilogoak. I did not see Uluksuk finish him. The other man ran away when he saw Ilogoak die. I asked Uluksuk, 'Is he dead?' and he said 'Yes, already.' I then said to Uluksuk, 'Give me the rifle.' He gave it to me; the first time I shot him I did not hit him, the second time I got him. The priest sat down when the bullet hit him. I went after him with a knife; when I was close to him he got up again; both of us were together, I had the knife in my hand, and I went after him when he got up again.

"Uluksuk told me, 'Go ahead and put the knife in him.' I said to Uluksuk, 'Go ahead you. I fixed the other man already.' The father fell down on his back. Uluksuk struck first with the knife and did not strike him; the second time he got him. The priest lay down and was breathing a little, when I struck him across the face with an axe I was carrying; I cut his legs with the axe; I killed him dead.

"After they were dead I said to Uluksuk, 'Before when white men were killed they used to cut off some and eat some.' Uluksuk cut up Ilogoak's belly; I turned around, Uluksuk gave me a little piece of the liver, I eat it; Uluksuk eat too.

"We covered up both bodies with snow when we started to go back."

With Sinnisiak's statement, the trial was practically at an end. The opposing lawyers made brief appeals to the jury, the prosecutor emphasizing the law and the completeness of the proof, the lawyer for the defence dwelling on the prisoner's ignorance of the laws which he infringed, and his fear that the priests would kill him. Silence then for a little space, broken at length by the voice of the Chief Justice, low but wholly distinct, in his charge to the jury. The guilt had been proved. The prisoner's fear of possible danger from the priests afforded no basis for the plea of self-defence. The Chief Justice's words were not so much a charge as an instruction. In the impassive eye of the law there would be only one verdict. Mitigation of that verdict, possible pardon for this primitive being, rested not with them, but with the Governor-General of Canada who would review the case.

The jury filed out, remained one hour, and returned. The clerk rose and asked for their verdict. The waiting crowd, swayed by the words of the judge, their sympathy for the accused temporarily overborne by a sense of the clearness of the law, expected but one verdict and that the single fatal word. But "Not guilty" were the words which came from the foreman's lips. Even the clerk doubted if he had heard aright, stumbled in his speech, and asked again. Once more the foreman repeated the verdict. There could be no doubt about it. To the jury, hard-headed men though they were, neither the law nor the evidence nor the chance of a subsequent pardon from Ottawa weighed in the balance with that pathetic anachronism, sitting hour after hour in the prisoner's box. And now that the verdict had been given, and the crowd was dispersing, the anachronism still sat there, staring dully into space. It was not until a guard touched him upon the shoulder and pointed down the private stairway leading to the guardroom that Sinnisiak, still unenlightened, went away.

The rest of the story can be very briefly told. A few days later a new trial was ordered with a change of *venue* to Calgary. On this occasion Sinnisiak and Uluksuk were tried together. The same scenes, the same lawyers, the same judge—but a new jury. The same evidence, the same witnesses —and in the prisoners' box two anachronisms instead of one. Sinnisiak's testimony was word for word as it was at Edmonton; Uluksuk's the same in essential detail as Sinnisiak's, and confirming the impression that Uluksuk was no more than a half unwilling accomplice. Again the jury were unequivocally instructed by the judge; but this time, less swayed by a sense of human values or perhaps more docile than their predecessors farther north, the jury rendered the verdict of guilty with a recommendation for mercy. Satisfied that the law had been vindicated, the judge did not even pass sentence, contenting himself with transmitting the recommendation to the Governor-General.

And then, lest anyone should imagine that the gulf between the stone age and the twentieth century had been bridged, the fates added the last touch of strangeness to the scene. "Tell them, Patsy," said the Chief Justice, "that they killed the priests and that they had no right to do it." But Patsy, erstwhile so ready, hesitated and was lost— lost somewhere in the mists that separate a taboo from a code of ethics. "No right"—what after all, did they know or had they learnt, of right? Again and again the judge tried to convey to them what all this should mean; and at length, with a form of words supplied by Inspector La Nauze, judge and jury and lawyers had to be content. "Tell them," said the Inspector to Patsy, "Big White Chief farther away than the distance you have been brought here, will say what is to be done, and maybe he won't be very hard on you, and this Chief will tell you what is going to be done to you soon when you get back to Edmonton."

Back to Edmonton, then, the two anachronisms were brought; and a few days later came the sentence from the "Big White Chief farther away." With the death penalty commuted to life imprisonment, Sinnisiak and Uluksuk, guarded by the indomitable patrol, set out on the long journey to Fort Resolution, where they were to be confined. The Law had been vindicated—and incidentally

Sinnisiak and Uluksuk had had their ride on the
Time Machine. Probably their consciences had not
been greatly educated by the experience; but at
least they had something to think over.

Two years later they were released and sent
home in the (perhaps not very well grounded) hope
that they could explain to their people the nature
of "right" and the ways of British justice.

II

A SIMPLE PERSON

IT IS not easy for us to-day, in the plentitude of printed literature, to conceive what life must have been in the Middle Ages, when "twenty bokes clad in blak or red" were all the learned clerk dared hope for, and when a hundred volumes constituted a plethoric library. To acquire such a library cost a fortune, and even a single volume was not to be had without lavish expenditure. Old Richard de Bury, who made a practice of exacting rare manuscripts of those who sought his favour with his master, Edward III, avers that "no dearness of price ought to hinder a man from the buying of books, if he has the money that is demanded for them"; and quaintly considers that the very bookshelves should be held sacred, as the rich setting of a precious jewel. "Moses, the gentlest of men, teaches us to make bookcases most neatly, wherein they may be protected from any injury: 'Take,' he says, 'this book of the law, and put it in the side of the ark of the covenant of the Lord your God.' O, fitting place and appropriate for a library, which was made of imperishable shittim-wood, and was all covered within and without with gold!"

No wonder the mediæval collector prized his book; for a single copy represented months and perhaps years of toil on the part of the monk in his

scriptorium or the scribe in his closet; and the very
slowness with which the text had been transcribed
warranted the expenditure of further years of toil
in the fitting decoration of it. This laboriousness
of production spelled rarity and costliness. Learning and culture, if not aristocratic, were at least
exclusive; and when, in the fruition of time, the
Renaissance came to loosen the intellectual bonds
of the Middle Ages, learning and culture would
still have remained the perquisites of wealth or of
religious seclusion, had it not been for one of those
timely miracles that illuminate the pages of history.

"In a silent laboratory," says M. Jusserand in
the prelude to his *Literary History of England in
the Renaissance,* "among blackened tables, surrounded by prentices who have sworn secrecy, the
master sets in line with patient hand small pieces
of metal; like an alchemist he seems, composing the
formula which will unlock the secret of gold. He
is as yet alone of his kind, his hand hesitates, and
his invention is incomplete; but he will act more
powerfully on the future of mankind than the in-
ventors of steam or of gunpowder. His craft has
no name of its own: he calls it 'the art of writing
artificially'."

Of these artisan-prophets, Faust and Gutenberg
had not yet achieved their *"monumentum aere
perennius,"* the great Gutenberg or Mazarin Bible,
and Aldus Manutius and Henri Estienne were not
yet born, when an English boy, native of Kent, and
speaking a dialect which he himself describes as

"broad and rude", left London, where he had been apprenticed to a mercer, and established himself in Bruges in the Low Countries. There, and in other parts of the Low Countries, Caxton continued, as he says in his first preface, for the space of thirty years. In Bruges he prospered, becoming, indeed, the first governor appointed by the Mercers' Association to pass upon all commercial problems arising through the transactions of the Mercers' Company. One might think that the busy merchant and commercial governor of Bruges would have had scant time for literature; but all his life Caxton seems to have been strangely haunted by the fear of that one of the Seven Deadly Sins from which we should imagine him most free. And so, in the year 1468, in order to exorcise the demon Idleness, he sets himself to translate (in long hand, of course,) a popular French compilation, *The Recuyell of the Histories of Troy.*

"When I remember," he explains in the Prologue to the completed work, "that every man is bounden by the commandment and counsel of the wise man to eschew sloth and idleness, which is mother and nourisher of vices, and ought to put himself unto virtuous occupation and business, then I, having no great charge of occupation, following the said counsel, took a French book, and read therein many strange and marvellous histories, wherein I had great pleasure and delight, as well for the novelty of the same as for the fair language of French, which was in prose so well and compendiously set and written, which methought I understood the sentence and substance of every matter. And for so much as this book was new and late made and drawn into French, and never had seen it in our English tongue, I thought in myself it should be a good business to translate it into our English, to the end that it might be had as well in the royaume of England as in other lands, and also for to pass therewith the time, and thus concluded in myself to begin this said work."

The translation thus undertaken to exorcise the demon Idleness, was laid aside after a time, because of the "simpleness and imperfectness" which Caxton confessed to, in both French and English. Meanwhile, he had given up his commercial activities and had entered into the household service of the Duchess of Burgundy, "the right high, excellent and right virtuous Princess, my right redoubted Lady, my Lady Margaret, by the grace of God, sister unto the King of England and of France." At her behest, he ingenuously explains, "whose dreadful commandment I durst in no wise disobey, because I am a servant unto her said Grace and receive of her yearly fee and other many good and great benefits and also hope many more to receive of her Highness," he devoted himself anew to the translation of the *Recuyell*. The translation prospered, but the translator waxed weary. The toil of writing out the text in the slow and precise script of the period began to tell upon Caxton; and the matter was further complicated by the appeals from many quarters for copies of the book. If one copy taxed him so heavily, how should he satisfy the noble gentlemen, his friends, who desired other copies?

The solution was at hand. Living at Bruges, he had heard talk of this new art of printing. Caxton was nothing if not thorough. Giving up everything else, he set himself to learn; and having learned he returned to the *Recuyell*, ready to satisfy his noble friends. "And forasmuch as in the writing of the same my pen is worn, my hand weary and not steadfast, mine eyne dimmed with overmuch looking on the white paper, and my courage not so prone and ready to labour as it hath been, and that age creepeth on me daily and feebleth all the body; and also because I have promised to divers gentlemen and to my friends to address to them as hastily as I might this said book, therefore, I have practised and learned at my great charge and dispense to ordain this said book in print after the manner and form as ye may here see, and is not written with pen and ink as other books be, to the end that every man may have them at once." And then follows an explanation which seems childish, until we look through Caxton's eyes. The long toil of completing a new copy of a manuscript meant that many months would intervene between the completion of one copy and the completion of the next. But now when the type was all set, a number of copies could be turned off on the same day. Wonderful! Caxton can hardly apprehend it himself. He feels that he ought to call public attention to the phenomenon. And so he adds: "For all the books (that is, copies) of this story, named *The Recuyell of the Histories of Troy*, thus imprinted as ye here see, were begun in one day and also finished in one day." And thus casually, being begun to avoid idleness, and being in this wise finished to save trouble, the first English book got itself printed. And thus, though not yet on English soil, was uttered the *fiat lux* in the creation of modern England.

For, casual as was the printing of the *Recuyell*, it had immediate and momentous consequences. Caxton forthwith translated into English and printed another book, *The Game and Playe of the Chesse*. By this time he had become wholly absorbed in his new occupation. He threw aside everything else, returned to England, set up his press beside or in Westminster Abbey, and on November 18th, 1477, printed the first English book ever struck off on English soil, *The Dictes and Sayings of the Philosophers*. It is not without significance that whereas Caxton's earlier printings had followed the practice of the time in making no reference to the date and the name of the printer, this book gives in the colophon Caxton's name, and the date and place of printing. It was worth while. Printing was started in England; and implicit in that crude machine at Westminster was the ceaseless activity of the modern presses, disseminating news and knowledge, stimulus and instruction,

wisdom and perhaps not a little folly as well,
throughout the English-speaking world.

From this 18th day of November, 1477, until his
death, fourteen years later, Caxton displayed the
most unexampled activity. He still refers now and
again in his prefaces to his desire to escape the
demon Idleness; but it is hard to see how he found
time even to eat and sleep. With his little corps of
assistants—never more than three and often only
one—he printed nearly eighty separate works, and,
including later editions of the same author, over
one hundred different books, or, on the whole, over
eighteen thousand pages. He himself translated
from French and Latin twenty-one books, and re-
vised the translations of many others. For each
of the works which came from his press he wrote a
preface, describing the circumstances which led him
to select it for publication, making comments which
sometimes amount to genuine critiques, and never
failing in his quaint and earnest way to point out
to the reader the moral profit which he may derive
from the perusal of the book. And through all these
prefaces run certain strongly marked personal char-
acteristics which help us to see the man not as a
mere mechanic, immortalized by a lucky chance,
and turned into dust five centuries ago, but as a
very vital, human, and personable man, not soon
to vanish from our ken.

And first of all is the simplicity, the *naïveté*, the
humility of his spirit. "I, William Caxton, simple
person"—so he describes himself in the preface to

the "Morte D'Arthur." "I laboured in the said translation after my simple and poor cunning"— is his favourite account of his work as a translator. For any faults in the work the author should not be held responsible. Instead, the reader should "arette it to my cunning which is full small in this behalf." He constantly refers to himself as "indigne and unworthy." No accumulation of epithets seems sufficient adequately to express his reverence for his mistress, the Duchess of Burgundy, whose fee he has received and whose further favours he ingenuously permits himself to expect. When Earl Rivers translates the *Dictes,* and Caxton proposes to print it, the "noble and puissant lord" suggests that Caxton should "oversee" the translation. He can hardly bring himself to take such a liberty and consents only after much urging. And when he undertakes to restore a passage which the noble translator has omitted, the printer is dismayed at the liberty which he contemplates, and sets himself, with quaint humour, to find excuses for the Earl's omission,—"forasmuch," he says, "as I am not certain whether it was in my Lord's copy or not, or else, peradventure, that the wind had blown over the leaf at the time of translation." And if any reader should not approve of Caxton's restoration, let him "rend the leaf out of the book." A book, too, which Caxton prints, however humble the printer, is designed to be read only by gentlemen. "It is not for a rude uplandish man to labour therein ne read it but only for a clerk and noble gentlemen. . . . For this book is not for every rude and uncunning man to see, but to clerks and very gentlemen that understand gentleness and science."

Side by side with this personal humility runs a strain of idealism—a steadfast stream, both fine and clear. The books which he selects for printing, even the romances, must be good for the soul. The *Golden Legend* shall be a "profit to all them that shall read or hear it read, and may increase in them virtue and expell vice and sin." The citizens of London are growing selfish. "There is almost none that intendeth to the common weal, but only every man for his singular profit"; and so, for their example and behoof, he prints a commentary on Cato, the noble Roman, because, says Caxton, "Unto the noble, ancient and renowned city, the city of London, in England, I, William Caxton, owe of right my service and good-will, and of very duty am bounden naturally to assist, aid, and counsel, as far forth as I can to my power, as to my mother of whom I have received my nurture and living." *Boethius* is reprinted in order that his readers may "learn to have and keep the better patience in adversities"; Malory's *King Arthur*, that the "noble lords and ladies and all other estates of what estate or degree they be of, may see and learn the noble acts of chivalry, the gentle and virtuous deeds that some Knights used in those days, humbly beseeching that they take the good and honest acts in their remembrance to follow the same, wherein they shall find many joyous and pleasant histories and noble and renowned acts of humanity, gentleness, and chivalry. For herein may be seen noble chivalry, courtesy, humanity, friendliness, hardyhood, love, friendship, cowardice, murder, hate, virtue, and sin. Do after the good and leave the evil, and it shall bring you to good fame and renown."

Nor would Caxton, in these imprintings, willingly do injustice to any man. He had printed Chaucer's *Canterbury Tales* from a version which he afterwards discovered to be inaccurate. When this matter was revealed to him, he hastened to make amends by printing a second edition of the *Canterbury Tales* from a better manuscript, and in so doing felt as lively a responsibility as if the old poet, dead nigh a hundred years, stood before him in the flesh. "I would endeavour me to imprint it again for to satisfy the author, whereas before by ignorance I erred in hurting and defaming his book in divers places, in setting in some things that he never said he made, and leaving out many things that he made which be requisite to be set in it."

Nor was Caxton an idealist only in the content of the books which he printed. The manner, too, gave him lively concern. In that day when prose was a mere tool, a clumsy medium, looked upon as the baser sister of poetry, undeserving of attention from the artist, Caxton had an ideal of prose style which, in aspiration if not in accomplishment, would have done credit to the stylists of a far later day. Chaucer he reverenced because the father of English poetry "embellished, ornated and made fair our English," which before his day was "rude and incongruous." But Chaucer's service was primarily to poetry; and Caxton, simple printer as he was, did what he could to ennoble the humbler medium of prose. He confesses that some critics have blamed him "saying that in my translations I had over curious terms, which could not be understood of common people," and that they have urged him to "use old and homely terms." To satisfy them, he has read old books as models of style; but "the English was so rude and broad that I could not well understood it." He laments the confusion of vocabulary and dialects in England—the lack of a uniform literary standard of English prose. "Certainly," he says, "it is hard to please every man because of diversity and change of language." Other "honest and great clerks" have advised him "to write the most curious terms" that he could find, "and thus between plain, rude, and curious I stand abashed." And so he resolves to write in a fashion "not over rude ne curious, but in such terms as shall be understood, by God's grace, according to my copy"—a sound and honest resolution, not unworthy of any man, in the twentieth century as in the fifteenth.

It was in the faithful practice of this resolution that Caxton spent many busy years of his old age at Westminster. When death called him in the year 1491, it chanced that he was at work printing a book entitled *The Art and Craft to know well how to die*. The close of his busy life is typical of the whole of it—a steadfast, honest, industrious man, earnestly endeavouring to do the work from day to day which Providence set before him—a simple-hearted printer, careless alike of glory and of material reward. The personality of the man is ideally summed up in an anecdote which he himself tells as an epilogue to his reprint of Æsop's *Fables*. A wealthy dean, visiting a little parish, came by chance upon an old friend of his who had remained but a simple parish priest. "I pray you," said the dean, "what is this benefice worth to you a year?" "Forsooth," said the good, simple man, "I wot never, for I make never account thereof how well I have had it four or five years!" "And know ye not," said he, "what it is worth? It should seem a good benefice." "No, forsooth," said he, "but I wot well what it shall be worth to me." "Why," said he, "what shall it be worth?" "Forsooth," said he, "if I do my true diligence in the cure of my parishioners in preaching and teaching, and do my part longing to my cure, I shall have heaven, therefore; and if their souls be lost, or any of them by my default, I shall be punished therefore, and hereof am I sure." And with that word the rich dean was abashed, and thought he should do the better and take more heed to his cures and benefices than he had done. And Caxton adds, "This was a good answer of a good priest and an honest."

AN ELIZABETHAN DIARIST

IT WAS in the pages of the Folio that *Twelfth Night* first found its way into print; but it is through the eyes of John Manningham that we first see it where Shakespeare meant us to see it—on the stage. The passage of Manningham's diary, kept while he was a student of the Middle Temple, in which he records his first and our first sight of *Twelfth Night*, has often been quoted, but will bear repetition:

"At our feast wee had a play called Twelve Night, or what you will, much like the commedy of errores, or Menechmi in Plautus, but most like and neere to that in Italian called *Inganni*. A good practise in it to make the steward beleeve his lady widdowe was in love with him, by counterfayting a letter as from his lady, in generall termes, telling him what shee liked best in him, and prescribing his gesture in smiling, his apparaile, Xc., and then when he came to practise making him beleeve they tooke him to be mad."

Every editor of *Twelfth Night* has mentioned or quoted this passage as the earliest record of a performance of the play; but, save for those who have turned the pages of Manningham's diary, Manningham himself remains the mere tag of a date. And yet, here is a *person* not wholly undiscoverable in the pages of his own jottings, who saw what most of us would barter a whole library of *biblia a biblia* to have seen. If Browning could be so moved by meeting one who had seen Shelley plain, surely John Manningham is worth a word or two.

I

Not much is known about him, outside the pages of the diary. His father Robert lived in Cambridgeshire, but it does not appear that John studied at either Cambridge or Oxford. He was entered of the Middle Temple on March 16th, 1598, kept his terms for seven years, and was called to the degree of an utter barrister on June 7th, 1605. His chamber-fellow was Edward Curle whose sister, Anne Curle, John Manningham married about the year 1607. On April 25th, 1612, he inherited the ample estates of a relative, Richard Manningham. John Manningham made his will on January 21st, 1622, and died not long afterwards, his will being admitted to probate in the same year.

To all intents, therefore, he lives for us only in the pages of his diary, kept more or less intermittently during twelve months of his residence at the Middle Temple. There is no such personal revelation as we get in Pepys, whose diary was his one intimate, and who felt as if it were to see himself "go into the grave" when he was compelled by failing eyesight to "resolve from this time forward to have it kept by my people in long hand, and must be contented to set down no more than is fit for them and all the world to know." John Manningham was not confessionally minded. He met interesting people, and jotted down what they said to him. He was near at hand when the great Queen died, and has left a record of that event which is valuable to the historian. He was an assiduous church-goer, and with a meticulous thoroughness made abstracts of the sermons. With no less appreciation, he noted the attempted witticisms, the quips and vulgar jests that passed current among his fellows of the Middle Temple. He copied down verses, most of them clumsy and dull. He was given to *facetiae,* but he was neither witty in himself nor the cause of wit in other men.

If, indeed, we could accept mere proportion as a criterion of his tastes, we should be forced to conclude that sermons were his chief concern. Within the brief period during which he kept a diary, Manningham made abstracts, some of them fairly long ones, of more than forty sermons. It is possible that he practised sermon-abstracting as an exercise profitable to the study of the law; it is possible that, in Stevenson's phrase, it was merely a proficiency that tempted him, and he practised to acquire it as men learn to whittle, in a wager with himself. Anyhow, this little diary is the most comprehensive repertory of Elizabethan sermons that the age has left to us.

Manningham was seldom a critical listener. The prominent Churchmen he usually reports at length and without comment, albeit with an occasional criticism on the manner of delivery: "At the Court at Whitehall—Dr. Thomson, Deane of Windsor made a sermon; he hath a sounding, laboured, artificial pronounciation; he regards that so much that his speech hath no more matter than needes in it." And of "Dr. Dawson of Trinity in Cambridge, at Paules Crosse His Text, VII, Isay. 10. All the while he prayed he kept on his velvet night cap until he came to name the Queene, and then off went that, when he had spoken before both of and to God with it on his head."

It may be assumed that Manningham, who was certainly not writing with an eye to posterity, did not think it necessary to describe the better-known preachers. But when an "irregular" came his way, he took a lively interest both in personality and in procedure: "At St. Clements—A plain plodding fellow, sometimes of Queens College in Cambridge, his text Heb. cap. XI, V8." "At Paules—One with a long browne beard, a hanging looke, a gloting eye, and a tossing learing jesture; his text 'Take heed of false prophets which come to you in sheeps clothing, but within are ravening wolves; you shall know them by their fruits'." "In the afternoon, at a church in Foster Lane end, one Clappam, a black fellow, with a sower look, but a good spirit, bold, and sometimes bluntly witty." "At the Black Friars—Mr. Egerton, a little church or chappel up stayres, but a great congregation, specially of women. After God be merciful, reade after the

second lesson; having sat a good tyme before in
the pulpit, willed them to sing to the glorie of God
and their own edifying, the 66 Psal, 2 part; after he
made a good prayer, then turned the glass, and to
his text, Acts vii, 23 & c."

Aside from the sermons, Manningham's diary
reflects primarily the contacts and the interests
natural to a student in the Middle Temple. Of
systematic study there is not a trace. Perhaps that
would be too much to expect of these casual jottings; but it is probable that there were no systemat-
atic studies to record. "Having spent some time in
studying upon the first elements and grounds of the
law", says Stow in the *Survey*, "they proceed to be
admitted, and become students in some of these
four houses or inns of court, where continuing by
the space of seven years or thereabouts, they frequent readings, meetings, boltings, and other
learned exercises, whereby growing ripe in the
knowledge of the laws, and approved withal to be of
honest conversation, they are . . . . selected and
called to the degree of utter barristers." Save for
one terse item—"I brought in a moote with Jo.
Bramstone"—there is no trace of the "readings,
meetings, boltings and other learned exercises" in
which he must have taken part; but he is careful to
record the names of those residents of the Inns of
Court who are from time to time "called by the
Queen" to be Sergeants; and apropos of such a list,
he adds: "It is said Mr. Snig offers 800 1. to be
Sergeant, whereupon Mr. Sergeant Harris said that

he doubted not but he should shortly salute his dear brother Mr. Snig. Argent makes Sargent." Not a trace of reprobation in the dry humour of John Manningham's punning aphorism. With all his propensity for theological discourse, argent would probably have made sargent for him too, had not the benefaction of his relative made a country gentleman of him instead.

It would take a lawyer, versed as well in the history of the law, to do justice to the documentary interest of John Manningham's diary. We must be content to catch between the lines a few glimpses of Manningham himself in his unprofessional moments. He emerges as very much the sort of person whom we should expect the average middle-class, moderately educated Elizabethan Englishman to be—a compound of credulity and practicality, of ignorance and shrewdness. He was given to record-ing strange medicaments for various ills, such as the extraordinary empiricism of the time afforded. He does not believe in Alchemy, but notes with amused interest the activities of the famous Nicholas Hill "a great profest philosopher," who numbered many of the great men of the day among his dupes. He is much impressed with what he has heard of "a cer-tain kind of compound called Laudanum . . . . very soveraign to mitigate any paine; it will for a time lay a man in a sweet trans, as Dr. Parry told me he tryed in a fever, and his sister Mrs. Turner in her childbirth." He is given to gossip, much of it scurrilous, and is fond of recording any sharp deal in money matters that comes to his ears. He has the sturdy prejudices of his class; is critical of the Scotch with their "lisping fumbling language," and explodes against the foreign affectations of travelled Englishmen, as vigorously if not as wittily as Rosalind did to Jacques. And how this redoubtable law student and Churchman despises the Puritans! "Such hypercrites are those professors," he exclaims. "A puritane," he notes, "is such an one as loves God with all his soul, and hates his neighbour with all his heart." He is ready to credit any story against them. "A Puritane schoolmaster that taught little children in their horne bookes would not have them say 'Christ crosse A,' but 'Black Spot A' ". And he draws a picture of a superstitious pastor which goes far to justify Ben Jonson's mordant study of the Reverend Tribulation Wholesome. This Puritan divine had lost his purse, and resorted to a "figure-caster" to discover the thief. "On the day appointed for the purpose, the other told him that when he caste a paper into the chaffing dish of coales which he placed before them, he should looke in the glass to see the visage of him that had it; but the flame being too short for him to advise well what face it was, he earnestly entreated to see it again. 'Oh,' said the other, 'I perceive well the cause why you could not discerne; it was that you trust too much in God.' 'Whoe, I', said the Puritan, 'I trust noe more in God than the post doth. Let me see it once againe.' "

It is curious to note in this connection that

Manningham numbered among his intimates in the
society of the Middle Temple young John Pym,
who later was to plead for the restoration of the
silenced Puritan divines, and who was destined to
become the great parliamentary leader in the
struggle against the king.

Indeed, Manningham's friends, and those with
whom his life in the Middle Temple brought him
into casual contact, include many notable figures.
Sir Thomas Overbury, poet and apostle of culture
in the court, for whom the fates had such a grimly
tragic doom in store; Sir John Davies, who had
already written his *Nosce Teipsum,* and of whom
our diarist speaks exceeding ill; "Jo. Bramstone,"
the future Lord Chief Justice; Sir Benjamin
Rudyard, poet and intimate friend of Ben Jonson,
were among his fellow-residents, and are often
quoted; he records a chat with Stow, the antiquary,
who talked to him about the recently published
"Survey" and, quoting his style of *Antiquarius
Angliae,* averred that "he was worthie of that title
for his paynes, for he hath noe gaines by his
travaile." The great Bacon, not yet even knighted
and but on the threshold of his career, and Sir
Walter Raleigh, recently back from his voyage to
the Azores, and enjoying a brief moment of calm
before the storm that was to burst upon him at the
accession of James, were familiar figures about the
purlieus of the Middle Temple. Anecdotes about
"Fr. Bacon" and "W. Rawley" abound in the
Diary; but of Bacon or Raleigh or any of the rest,

Manningham affords us not one right describing word. It was not that he altogether lacked the power to catch a likeness. We venture to think that his picture of the preacher at Paul's, with his long brown beard, his hanging look, his gloating eye and his tossing, learing gesture sufficiently shows the diarist's powers. But it simply did not occur to him (any more, alas, than it usually occurs to us in our own jottings) to commit to paper the familiar and the obvious. What in truth were the

"Words that wise Bacon or brave Raleigh spoke"

in their hours of ease? With what quick gesture did Bacon point his aphorisms? How did Raleigh look, what tricks of manner had he, as he came swaggering up in peacock plumage from his house in the Strand? When shall we ever learn that the *trivia* of one generation are sure to become the treasures of the next? And by what perversity of fate should a man who was a contemporary of John Marston and Ben Jonson and William Shakespeare and who must have seen them as often as Manningham did in that play-going little town of London— by what perversity of fate should our diarist name these very three only to tell a more or less discreditable story about each one of them?

II

It is, however, a later entry in the diary that couples Shakespeare's name with Burbage's in an

anecdote of amorous rivalry. But on the occasion
of the performance of *Twelfth Night,* no names are
mentioned. If only the vagrant spirit of Charles
Lamb could have found prior lodgment in the
breast of this easy-going Elizabethan, what a feast
we should have had! There is no play which we
should so wish to see through Elizabethan eyes as
Twelfth Night. There is no setting, no, not even
the wooden O of the Globe itself, so alluring as that
beautiful old Hall of the Middle Temple. There is
no group of Elizabethans whom we should so like
to summon in bodily presence as "the L. Chamber-
leyne his servants" including those "principal
Comedians, Will. Shakespeare, Aug. Philips, Hen.
Condell, Will. Kempe, Ric. Burbadge, Joh. Hem-
ings, Tho. Pope, Chr. Beeston, Joh. Dyke." Nothing short of the most irrefutable documentary
evidence ought to shake our belief that on that
occasion Will. Kempe played Sir Andrew Ague-
cheek and Ric. Burbadge played Sir Toby Belch and
Will. Shakespeare played Malvolio. There is nobody among those ancillary figures who contribute
their touches of reality to the scene who had such a
chance at immortality as worthy John Manningham. But if the exasperating fellow disregards his
obligation to posterity and simply refuses to play
up for us, we must read between the lines.

The grave dignity of the noble old Gothic Hall
of the Middle Temple somehow commends itself as
a setting for the romantic beauty and riotous fun
of *Twelfth Night.* There is a kind of whimsical

effrontery about the whole affair. High overhead, so high that the players on the stage at one end of the hall are dwarfed by it, spreads the beautiful open-work ceiling of time-darkened oak. ๏ Full length paintings of princes of the blood look gravely down upon the antics of these "rogues and vagabonds." Armorial bearings of the Knights Templar, emblazoned upon the windows, commemorate the glory of a mediaeval dream. Built though it was only half a century before Manningham played his little part, it has wholly blended with the ancient pile, and from the near-by Temple Church with its blackened effigies armoured ghosts come to haunt the shadows. "What country, friend, is this?" asks Viola as, all semblative a woman's part, she trips forward on the stage. "This is Illyria, Lady," replies the Sea-Captain.

John Manningham, we may guess, was somewhat insensitive to ghosts; and if the verses which he quotes in the diary are a fair criterion of his taste, he was none too responsive to Viola's loyal cantons of contemned love. A sweet youth, no doubt, this Viola, and a pretty turn of words. But Will. Kempe as Sir Andrew, displaying all the good gifts of nature, and no doubt speaking more than is set down for him; and Ric. Burbadge as Sir Toby, drinking till his brains turn o' the toe like a parish-top—this is something like. A little more of this, my masters, and honest John Manningham himself will go to church in a galliard and come home in a coranto. As for Viola, no doubt she will win her duke in the end. They all do in these Italian stories that are now so popular.

But here, in sooth, is a less conventional story, that seems to be getting off to a good start. Will. Shakespeare is on the stage. "Ho!" says John Manningham, " 'A kind of Puritan,' the wench calls him. And 'sick of self love' ". He gives an approving nod, is reminded of a story anent these "silly hypocrites," and imparts it to his neighbour. "Whist, man," calls Thomas Overbury from a bench behind, "you are spoiling the play." John Manningham settles back with a grunt, to savour at his leisure the outcome of this cony-catching trick played on the puritanical Malvolio, and resolves to write out the story of the Steward and his Lady Widdowe in his diary before he goes to bed.

And here we leave him, not sorry on the whole that he was only an ordinary sort of person. He is rather more real for that. Around his solid commonplaceness, the insubstantial pageant becomes for the moment a little less shadowy. The sergeants at law in their parti-coloured robes and capes "furred with lamb"; the junior counsellors in their pleated gowns of "a sad colour"; but all, as Manningham records, "so filled with pride and fantastickness, that every one must have a velvet face, and be tricked with lace"; the students in their robes of sober black; visitors decked in the extraordinary diversity of costume characteristic of the time—great padded doublets glistening with gold and silver lace, French or Venetian hose, silk stockings, shoes gleaming with gold or silver buckles—apes of every continental fashion. John Manningham, bestirring himself on a convivial errand, turns in the doorway to look back. The glittering costumes, individually distinct near at hand, blend into a mere riot of colour down the perspective of the great hall. Untouched by the pathos of Malvolio's explanation, our diarist shoulders his way out. "To be sure!" he says to himself, "That's the way to treat a Puritan—

'The most notorious geck and gull
That e'er invention play'd on'."

DEAR FINE SILLY OLD ANGEL

THOMAS FULLER'S folios have long since been broken up into numerous volumes; but, even in this more usable form, they still make what Lamb called "massy reading", and to the pleasure-seeker their titles are as forbidding as their bulk. What reader would turn for delectation to six volumes of a *Church History* or three stout volumes (the *Worthies*) filled with half-page biographies of persons whose candle flickered out more than three centuries ago? Or who would seek lively reading in a collection of "Characters", illustrating "The Good Wife", "The Good Husband", "The Good Widow", "The Good Landlord", and more, under the heading of *The Holy State*? Surely these must be (the words are Fuller's) mere "auxiliary books, only to be repaired-to on occasions", or even "such as are mere pieces of formality, so that if you look *on* them you look *through* them; and he that peeps through the casement of the index, sees as much as if he were in the house".

And then some light-hearted adventurer essays to turn a page or two of Fuller for the adventure's sake. Be it the *Church History,* or the *Worthies,* or *The Holy State,* or the *History of Cambridge,* or the *Pisgah-sight of Palestine,* or any one of half-a-dozen of the minor things, he discovers that no

subject is so solemn or so dry, no compilation of a
biography is so commonplace, but Fuller will
lighten it with his gaiety, or mellow it with his
charity, or irradiate it with his wit, or twist it with
a quaint conceit. The sentence on "auxiliary books"
is representative—and who but Fuller would have
peeped through the casement of the index?

Such a discovery may be made on any page; but
relish for the unexpected, the sudden sally, the
delightful irrelevance, is a matter of temperament.
Most of Fuller's contemporaries liked him enorm-
ously. It was an age of verbal gymnastics and
quick conceits. They liked puns, and Fuller was
the most inveterate of punsters. Nor did they
prize him merely for his tricks. They liked him
because he could be at once wise and merry. There
was not much merriment in the years between the
appearance of Fuller's *Holy State* in 1642 and his
death on the 16th of August, 1661. His genial
books, masking under solemn titles, went to many
editions in those years. There is a delightful
glimpse, which Oldys gives us in a seventeenth-
century *Medley of diverting Sayings, Stories, Characters, etc.*, of a meeting between Fuller and Isaak
Walton. Walton, too, liked to mix in what he
wrote "some innocent harmless mirth; of which,
if thou be a severe, sour-complexioned man, then
I here disallow thee to be a competent judge".
Walton, so the story goes, visited Fuller to secure
materials for the life of Richard Hooker. The
Church History had just appeared.

"What do you think of it?" asked Fuller.

"I think," replied Walton, "that it should be acceptable to all tempers, because there are *shades* in it for the warm, and *sunshine* for those of a cold constitution. With youthful readers, the facetious parts will be profitable to make the serious more palatable, while reverend old readers will fancy themselves in a flower garden, or one full of evergreens."

"And why not the Church History so decked," said Fuller, "as well as the Church itself at a most Holy Season, or the Tabernacle of old at the Feast of Boughs?"

"That was but *for a season,*" Walton objected. "In *your* Feast of Boughs, we are so overshadowed that the parson is more seen than.his congregation; who may wander till they are lost in the labyrinth."

"Oh," said Fuller, "the very *children* of our Israel may find their way out of *this* wilderness."

"True," returned Walton, "as indeed they have here such a Moses to conduct them."

There are many such indications of contemporary liking for "the great Tom Fuller". Pepys pored over the *Church History* (while Mistress Pepys was deep in "Great Cyrus") till late at night; or, after debating at his bookseller's on the claims of Chaucer, Stow, Shakespeare, or Jonson, "at last chose Dr. Fuller's *Worthies*", and spent next Easter day at home with his wife in "pleasant talk and company one with another reading in Dr. Fuller's book".

But in that day as in this there were not lacking severe sour-complexioned men who had no patience with a playful spirit. Dr. Heylin condemned Fuller's "merry tales and scraps of Trencher-jests", which "neither do become the gravity of a Church-historian, nor are consistent with the nature of a sober argument". Bishop Nicholson said that the *Church History* was "so interlac'd with Punn and Quibble, that it looks as if the Man had design'd to ridicule the Annals of our Church into Fable and Romance", but added that "if it were possible to refine it well, the work would be of good use".

In the eighteenth century Oldys thought that "Dr. Fuller had some elegancies of style, but he indulged them till they diseased it"; Bishop Warburton called him "Fuller the Jester" and said that he wrote "in a style of buffoon pleasantry altogether unsuitable to so grave and important a subject". Even as late as 1810 a writer in the *Edinburgh Review* thinks that Fuller's "quaint and antiquated wit is perhaps more frequently found to disgust than to delight a fashionable age".

The *Edinburgh Review* was wrong. In the 1790's the *Gentleman's Magazine* began to quote Fuller and to suggest that there should be new editions. Southey professed that Fuller was his "prime favourite author", and enriched his Commonplace Books with copious extracts from *The Holy State* and the *Church History* and the *Worthies*. Then came Lamb, in whose merry and wayward fancy Fuller himself was reborn. It is not for nothing that the two writers to whom their contemporaries and posterity have applied the word "quaint" are Fuller and Charles Lamb. "He was very kind, as he always was to young people, and very quaint", wrote one who as a boy had fallen under Lamb's spell. "I told him that I had devoured his 'Roast Pig'. He congratulated me on possessing a thorough schoolboy's appetite." It is what Fuller might have said, and just what would have been said about him. It was Lamb (introducer of so many riches to the early nineteenth century) who first made Fuller generally known. Lamb's *Specimens from the Writings of Thomas Fuller* (taken chiefly from *The Holy State*) appeared in Leigh Hunt's *Reflector* in 1811. The same year saw the publication of John Nichols' reprint of the *Worthies*—and Fuller came into his own again.

Then Coleridge caught the infection (his notes are dated July 1829); and Lamb, stirred to renewed interest, borrowed the *Worthies* from Coleridge and rejoiced over it in letters to Gillman and Barton. Fuller delighted Lamb; Coleridge was roused to enthusiasm. "Next to Shakespeare", he wrote, "I am not certain whether Thomas Fuller, beyond all other writers, does not excite in me the sense and emotion of the marvellous: the degree in which any given faculty or combination of faculties is possessed and manifested, so far surpassing what one would have thought possible in a single mind, as to give one's admiration the flavour and quality of wonder! . . . Fuller was incomparably the most *sensible,* the *least* prejudiced, great man of an age that boasted a galaxy of great men. He is a very voluminous writer, and yet in all his numerous volumes on so many different subjects, it is scarcely too much to say, that you will hardly find a page in which some one sentence out of every three does not deserve to be quoted for itself, as motto or as maxim. *God bless thee,* dear old man! May I meet with thee! which is tantamount to—may I go to Heaven!"

It may be doubted whether Coleridge was not moved to undue enthusiasm. We hesitate to rank Fuller's power as next to Shakespeare's in exciting the sense of the marvellous. The significance of Coleridge's outburst is that no one can read Fuller without loving him. Coleridge's "dear old man"; Lamb's "dear fine silly old angel"; the "quaint old Fuller" of every enthusiastic discoverer, mark a human and endearing quality. Among all English writers only Lamb is so self-revealing. When we turn the opening pages of any book of Fuller's, we are amused *at* him; as we read on, we are amused *with* him; but by the time we have turned the last page, he will have us by the heart-strings. His ingenuity entertains, but it is his ingenuousness that captivates. He will sacrifice anything—proportion, relevance, continuity, anything but decency —for a good story. He knows his besetting sin, and, in the act of sinning, he exclaims: "Forgive me, reader, though I would not write these things they are so absurd, I cannot but write them they

are so absurd." Or again: "Reader, if the day be
as long with thee when thou readest, as it was with
me when I wrote, the ensuing story, time may be
the better afforded for the perusal thereof."

It is characteristic too of his ingenuous spirit
that even in graver matters he never hesitates to
take the reader into his confidence. In that
troubled time all men who were not zealots or
fanatics wished, as Fuller did, to "tread fair and
softly"; but there were few so engagingly frank
about it. Church history, as it approached his own
day, became dangerous ground, comments on the
notable controversialists of the day a delicate matter. "To say much in praise or dispraise of them
(wherein their relations are so nearly concerned)
may add too much to the writer's danger" is a
thought that in one form or another falls frequently
from Fuller's pen. These deliberate evasions, and
the fact that he suffered less during the Common-
wealth than many Royalist divines, exposed him to
the charge of pusillanimity and "trimming"; but in
truth Fuller's life was an open book. "Had I
poised myself so politickly betwixt both parties
that I had suffered from neither", he writes in his
Good Thoughts in Bad Times, "yet could I have
took no contentment in my safe escaping." He
was unswervingly faithful to his King and his
Creed; but peace, conciliation, tolerance, good feeling, were his watchwords. The *Appeal of Injured
Innocence,* in which he replies to Heylin's bitter
attack on the *Church History,* is an example of

sustained good temper and genial humour remarkable in an age when theological controversy descended to ignoble personalities. As for the letter "To my Loving Friend, Dr. Peter Heylin", which concludes the *Appeal,* Fuller's very self, quaint, gentle, kindly, is compact in it. It is true that, man of his time, Fuller disliked the Catholics. To write impartially of them would have been to neglect his duty as a good Churchman. He pointed many a moral, and indulged in many a gibe, at their expense. He felt no inconsistency in crediting the miracle of the King's Evil and at the same time discrediting the miracles of the *Legenda Aurea.* But, not infrequently, his liberal spirit gets the better of his professional prejudice. "As for miracles which she wrought in her life-time", he writes of St. Hildegarde, "their number is as admirable as their nature. I must confess, at my first reading of them, my belief digested some, but surfeited on the rest: for she made no more to cast out a devil, than a barber to draw a tooth, and with less pain to the patient. . . . However, Hildegardis was a gracious virgin, and God might perform some great wonders by her hand."

It is not easy to do Fuller justice in a volume of selections. To collect his *obiter dicta*; to display him in cap and bells; to adopt Heylin's ironic suggestion that his "merry tales and scraps of Trencherjests" be "put into a book by themselves" and "served up for a second course to the *Banquet of Jests,* a supplement to the old book entitled *Wits,*

Fits and Fancies, or an additional century to the old *Hundred Merry Tales*, so long since extant", would be to miss the best of him. Lamb's selections do little more than illustrate the liveliness of Fuller's fancy. Coleridge's "one sentence out of every three . . . as motto or maxim" suggests the scrapbook. In such oddments Fuller's whimsical charm evaporates. His books, in truth, are good talk, the spontaneous overflow of a merry mind— and good talk requires leisure and a setting.

MR. RICHARDSON ARRIVES

"MR. RIVINGTON and Mr. Osborne to see you, Sir."

The servant's announcement ended his reverie. After a long day in the printing house, he had counted on a quiet evening. His fiftieth birthday had seemed a good time for taking stock. He had been looking back over those fifty years—his childhood in the little Derbyshire village; his seven years of 'prenticeship to Master John Wilde of Stationers' Hall; his start for himself in Fleet Street; his slow rise to affluence as a master-printer; his pride in his honest tradesman life. He was enjoying his retrospect. He grudged the interruption, not foreseeing how fraught with possibilities this evening was to be.

Old friends, these visitors—fellow-printers whose rivalry in the trade had not affected their friendship for honest Mr. Richardson. Twenty years before, Charles Rivington had taken over Richard Chiswell's publishing business at the Rose and Crown, Paul's Churchyard, and had built up a substantial connection as printer of theological works. He had brought out one of Whitefield's earliest books, *The Nature and Necessity of a New Birth in Christ,* and Wesley's edition of *Thomas à*

Kempis. He was to be the founder of a House. For more than a century a Rivington was to preside over it. One of his sons was to emigrate, become King's Printer for New York, publish *Rivington's New York Loyal Gazette,* print Major André's *Cow Chase,* and ultimately figure as a spy in the pay of General George Washington. A grandson was to publish standard editions of Shakespeare, Milton and Locke. A great-grandson was to figure in the Tractarian movement as publisher of *Tracts for the Times* and Newman's *Parochial Sermons.* Charles Rivington, Richardson's friend, was a man of parts and breeding. They had not been intimates. Richardson was a creature of his class, and never really emancipated himself. In Rivington there was a touch of the aristocrat. But they trusted each other. When Rivington died, Richardson became executor and guardian for Rivington's thirteen children.

Thomas Osborne was of different calibre. He was reputed at once the most illiterate and the most successful bookseller in London. The next few years were to provide him with two bids for a vicarious immortality. Pope, angry because Osborne was selling subscription copies of his *Iliad* for half price, substituted him for Chalmers in the 1742 edition of *The Dunciad.*

And Johnson knocked him down. According to Johnson, Osborne was "destitute of shame". "I have beat many a fellow, but the rest had the wit to hold their tongues", said the Great Cham to his "dearest lady", Mrs. Piozzi. It is a debatable question whether the other fellows did well to hold their tongues. Perhaps, gentle reader, one of your ancestors was numbered among that headlong company. Had he spoken, he too might have been recorded in Boswell's pages:

"Named and known by that moment's feat;
There took his station and degree."

Only the name would have been necessary. Dame Rumour would have done the rest. She was not niggardly in her treatment of Osborne. One version had it that he was knocked down in his shop and the magisterial foot placed upon his neck. Johnson averred that it happened in his own chamber. Thereupon, once more, Rumour set the stage. Osborne was standing on a ladder. The lethal weapon which hurled him flaming from the etherial sky was the Dictionary.

Johnson said that Osborne was "a blockhead"; but in Osborne's hard head an idea had germinated. That, in fact, was why Mr. Rivington and Mr. Osborne had broken in upon Richardson's quiet evening. Rivington remained in the background. Osborne put the case. There would be, he believed, a fair sale for a little book of model letters, nothing nice or pretentious, plain things really, the sort country people without much schooling would like to have by them when they had to write a letter

and didn't just know how to do it. Mr. Rivington
and he had supped together. The matter had been
discussed between them. He himself didn't pretend
to know a good letter from a bad one. He did his
business by word of mouth and when a letter had
to be written his clerks did it for him. But Mr.
Richardson had written prefaces to some of the
books he had printed. And Mr. Rivington had
seen (Osborne smacked his lips over the phrase)
some of Mr. Richardson's epistolary compositions.
Mr. Rivington thought that Mr. Richardson was
the man to do it. They had come together to pro-
pose it. *Would* Mr. Richardson do it? If so, Mr.
Rivington and he would print it, and he, Thomas
Osborne, would make it sell.

Mr. Richardson listened and meditated. His
thoughts went back to his boyhood when he used
to write letters for love-lorn village maids. How
often they had opened their hearts to him, de-
pended upon him for the delicate art of addressing
to a rustic swain a No that might become a Yes,
or of chiding without repulsing an over-forward
lover! He bethought him too of the middle-aged
widow, pious but scandalmongering, to whom, in
the guise of eld, he had written a letter of admoni-
tion, fortified with sundry Scripture texts. She had
identified his hand-writing, complained with tears
to his mother. His wise old mother had chidden
him—but gently, he remembered, assuring him
that his principles were right but that it would be

better to wait a while before giving unasked advice
to grown-up people. He was old enough now certainly—

"Will it be any harm," said he to Osborne, "in
a piece you want to be written so low, if we should
instruct them how they should think and act in
common cases, as well as indite?" "Harm? No,"
said blunt Osborne. " 'Twill make the book sell
better."

His callers departed. Already his mind teemed
with occasions and predicaments. "Recommending
a superior Manservant"; "Recommending a Wet-
nurse"; "Recommending a Cook-maid"; "Recommending a Chamber-maid"; "Recommending a
Nursery-maid";—obvious, these. His thoughts
raced past them. Instruct his readers how they
should think and act in common cases—there lay
the real opportunity. "From a Maid-servant in
Town, acquainting her Father and Mother in the
Country with a Proposal of Marriage, and asking
their Consents"; "From a tender Father to an un-
gracious Son"; "From a respectful Lover to his
Mistress"; "Advice from a Father to a young
Beginner, what Company to choose, and how to
behave in it";—possibilities these, worth experi-
menting with to-morrow. Memories of his own
'prentice days: "From an Apprentice to an Uncle,
about a Fraud committed by his Fellow-Appren-
tice"; "From an Apprentice to his Master, begging
Forgiveness for a great Misdemeanour"; "From an

Apprentice to his Friends, in Praise of his Master and Family". He dwelt on that for a little and paused to devise a phrase or two:

"Who can but love such a family? I wish, when it shall please God to put me in such a station, that I may carry myself just as my master does; and, if I should ever marry, have just such a wife as my mistress."

Why, there were no limits to the possibilities in such a book. Anonymous letters, even! Proper warnings, of course, "by the hand of a friend". Several of them, perhaps, showing how the thing might be done with decorum and with nice gradations of severity. And why content himself with single letters? Why not imagine whole successions of contingencies, and provide the proper letter for each? "A Gentleman to a Lady, professing an Aversion to the tedious Forms of Courtship"; "The Lady's Answer, encouraging a farther Declaration"; "The Gentleman's Reply, more explicitly avowing his Passion"; "The Lady's Answer to his Reply, putting the Matter on a sudden Issue"—he went to sleep, devising them.

He got at it next morning, and for a month or two did little else. And then, one day, as he sat re-reading the model letter which he had just completed, something happened to him. In his careful script he had entitled the letter: "A Father to a Daughter in Service, on hearing of her Master's attempting her Virtue." He had written:

"My dear Daughter,

"I understand, with great grief of heart, that your master has made some attempts on your virtue, and yet that you stay with him. God grant that you have not already yielded to his base desires! For when once a person has so far forgotten what belongs to himself, or his character, as to make such an attempt, the very continuance with him, and in his power, and under the same roof, is an encouragement to him to prosecute. And if he carries it better, and more civil, at present, it is only the more certainly to undo you when he attacks you next. Consider, my dear child, your reputation is all you have to trust to. And if you have not already, which God forbid! yielded to him, leave it not to the hazard of another temptation; but come away directly (as you ought to have done on your own motion) at the command of

"Your grieved and indulgent Father."

Where had he heard something like that? It came back, the tale that someone had told him years ago—of a country girl who had gone out to service in a County Family. The son of the house, foiled in persistent attempts to seduce her, had at length conceived a just esteem for her character and had married her. Social elevation the reward of virtue. A Story.

He laid aside the Model Letters—and *Pamela* came. In his methodical way, he noted on the first page of the manuscript of *Pamela*: "Begun Nov. 10, 1739," and on the last page, "Finished, Jan. 10, 1739-40." That First Part (he was to write a second of like length) ran to 200,000 words—Sundays off, toward 4,000 words a day. His "inspired ink-horn" was to flow like that for about fifteen years. He suffered from a chronic "dizziness in the head" and "mistiness in the eyes". "I cannot tell why," he recorded, "but my nervous disorders will permit me to write with more impunity than to read." He gave up reading. He appeared less frequently at his printing house. He became the veritable Man of Letters. Having by the sheer chance of Osborne's suggestion adopted the letter-form, he persisted in it. When he was not thus developing the plots of his "fictitious adventures", he was with the same meticulous care, composing voluminous replies to his correspondents. He preserved their letters and copies of his replies. As the letters poured in on him, the quiet little man, sitting there in his shadowy study, like a little fat spider weaving a web of plots, came to realize what he was accomplishing.

To readers of the 1740's, the mere fact that a maid-servant could be made the heroine of a readable "romance" was startling enough. The romances of Calprenède and Scudéri, with their highborn ladies and high-flown rhetoric, were still setting the pace—romances which Mrs. Pepys had inflicted upon her rebellious husband in the coach; which Addison had found occupying the place of honour in Leonora's library; which the Baron in *The Rape of the Lock* had made the foundation of his Altar of Love. Brilliant young Hester Mulso, who became "the celebrated Mrs. Chapone", had "dragged through *Le Grand Cyrus* in twelve huge volumes; *Ibrahim, Clélie*, and some others, whose names, as well as the rest of them, I have forgotten." Even hard-headed Samuel Johnson had "read them all".

But here was a plain country girl, destitute of rank and rhetoric, whose fictitious adventures and niceties of conscience captured the attention. Honest Goodman Andrews! Ingenuous, long-suffering, richly rewarded Pamela! Stern, selfish Mr. B——! Proud, passionate Lady Davers! Odious Mrs. Jewkes! The public took them to their hearts. First published in November, 1740, *Pamela* reached a fourth edition by May, 1741. An epigrammatist, "after reading *Pamela*," delivered himself of this "Advice to Booksellers":

"Since printers with such pleasing nature write,
And since so awkwardly your scribes indite,
Be wise in time and take a friendly hint;
Let printers write, and let your writers print."

By November, 1741, James Dance had turned it into a comedy for the London stage, and Abbé Prévost had translated it into French: *Paméla; ou la Vertu recompensée. Traduit de l'Anglais. En deux tomes. A Londres chez T. Woodward. pr. 6s.*

Aaron Hill and Richardson had corresponded for many years before *Pamela* was published.

Aaron's grandiloquent plays had not fared any too
well on the London stage. Richardson had been
unfailingly sympathetic. Aaron had three grown
daughters, Urania, Astraea and Minerva. Minerva,
unfortunately, was known to her intimates as
"Minnie," but Urania and Astraea conscientiously
lived up to their names. To Urania and Astraea,
Richardson sent the two volumes of *Pamela*, fresh
from the press. Urania and Astraea were "quite
filled and transported with the triumphs of Pamela." They replied "as soon as they could find their
hearts at ease enough to tell their transports." The
effect upon Aaron himself was overwhelming:

"I have done nothing but read it to others and
hear others again read it to me, ever since it came
into my hands; and I find I am likely to do nothing
else, for the Lord knows how long yet to come; because if I lay the book down it comes after me.
When it has dwelt all day long upon the ear, it
takes possession all night of the fancy. It has witch-
craft in every page of it."

Most encomiasts would have let it go at that;
but Aaron had a card yet to play. The Hills had
adopted Harry Campbell, six years old, "son of an
honest, poor soldier, by a wife, grave, unmeaning
and innocent." Aaron was reading *Pamela* aloud
to "some company". Harry:

"crept under my chair, and was sitting before me
on the carpet, with his head almost touching the

book, and his face bowing down towards the fire. He had sat for some time in this posture, with a stillness that made us conclude him asleep; when on a sudden we heard a succession of heart-heaving sobs, which, while he strove to conceal from our notice, his little sides swelled as if they would burst, with the throbbing restraint of his sorrow. I turned his innocent face to look towards me, but his eyes were quite lost in his tears; which, running down from his cheek in free currents, had formed two sincere little fountains on that part of the carpet he hung over. All the ladies in company were ready to devour him with kisses, and he has since become doubly a favourite; and is, perhaps, the youngest of Pamela's converts."

Though sentimental Hills raved over *Pamela*, and lachrimose children deposited sincere little fountains upon sundry carpets, and the Reverend Dr. Slocock recommended it from his pulpit of St. Saviour's, and even cynical Mr. Pope said that *Pamela* "would do more good than many volumes of sermons," there were, it must be admitted, scoffers. The arch-scoffer, of course, was Henry Fielding. Wicked Mr. Fielding saw through the whole business. "Sweet, dear, pretty" Pamela had in fact played her cards rather well. "The matchless arts of that young politician" are wittily exposed in *An Apology for the Life of Mrs. Shamela Andrews*. Parson Oliver is a neighbour of the Andrews family. When Parson Tickletext sends him a copy of *Pamela*, explaining that in London "the pulpit as well

as the coffee-house hath resounded with its praise",
Parson Oliver waxes righteously indignant. Shamela, he replies, was a baggage, and here are some
of her real letters to prove it. The letters are ingenious parodies of Pamela's, with just enough
twist to make her wiles palpable.

From *Shamela,* as all the world knows, Fielding
proceeded to *Joseph Andrews,* in which an intended
burlesque of *Pamela* develops into the first of his
great novels. Richardson plumed himself that:

"the *Pamela* which [Fielding] abused in his *Shamela* taught him how to write to please, though his
manners are so different. Before his *Joseph Andrews* (hints and names taken from that story, with
a lewd and ungenerous engraftment), the poor man
wrote without being read;"

but Richardson never forgave Fielding for the
double affront. To Sarah Fielding, Richardson
said:

"Had your brother been born in a stable, or been
a runner at a sponging-house, we should have
thought him a genius, and wished he had had the
advantage of a liberal education, and of being admitted into good company; but it is beyond my
conception, that a man of family, and who had
some learning, and who really is a writer, should
descend so excessively low."

Low as *Tom Jones* was, Richardson did not hesitate to commission Astraea and Minerva to read

it for him. He had not, he declared, read it himself. But the Goddess of Justice and the Goddess
of Wisdom, having "got over some reluctance that
was bred by a familiar coarseness in the title", had
the audacity to report that they had read "the whole
six volumes, and found much masqued merit in
'em all; a double merit both of heart and head."
That did for Astraea and Minerva.

Meanwhile, Richardson went steadfastly on. He
resumed and finished, and Rivington printed, and
Osborne and James Leake of Bath sold, the *Letters
Written to and for Particular Friends, On the most
Important Occasions, Directing not only the Re-
quisite Style and Forms to be Observed in Writing
Familiar Letters; but How to Think and Act Justly
and Prudently in the Common Concerns of Human
Life.* Spurred by a continuation, *Pamela in High
Life,* written by an anonymous rival, he wrote two
more volumes, describing Pamela's struggles to
adapt herself to County Society, as the wife of Mr.
B——. And then he conceived, still in his dogged
letter-form, his masterpiece, *Clarissa Harlowe.*

Was there ever a story that could be summarized
so briefly, and that took so many words to tell?
Clarissa, importuned by her parents to marry rich
but unattractive Mr. Solmes, accepts the assurance
of the fascinating Lovelace that he will provide her
safe retreat with his family, and runs away with
him. Lovelace takes her to a house of ill-fame and
ruins her. She dies, refusing the repentant Love-

lace's offer of honourable marriage. A relative of
Clarissa's kills Lovelace in a duel. Sixty-five words.
What with Clarissa's letters to *her* confidante, and
Lovelace's letters to *his* friend, and sundry other
letters, the story runs to nearly 900,000 words.

Was it Richardson's shrewdness, or merely his
rate of composition, that caused the issue of *Clarissa* in two parts—the first four volumes in the
early spring of 1748, the last three in the late
autumn of the same year? Those first four volumes
brought Clarissa into Lovelace's clutches—and left
her there. Clarissa is cast off by her family, pub-
licly known to be in Lovelace's keeping. He will
marry her; he will even draw up formal marriage
settlements: "but by my soul, Belford, her haughti-
ness shall be brought down to own both love and
obligation to me." Even to the jaded and cynical
modern reader that fourth volume is curiously compelling. Lovelace will seduce her before he will
marry her. The whole thing is preposterous, in-
credible. No human being could ever have devised
such stratagems, suborned such a multitude of
agents, successfully brought off such a variety of
situations. Seduction becomes a punctilio, and the
art of seduction is elevated to a place among the
fine arts. It is all utterly ridiculous—and yet,
somehow, Clarissa transcends these absurdities—
helpless, defiant Clarissa, daunting Lovelace's ap-
proaches by the sheer strength of her virginal purity.

Lovelace will win. Clarissa will be shamed.

Richardson made that clear in the fourth volume.
Then came the letters:

"I am pressed, Sir, by a multitude of your admirers, to plead in behalf of your amiable Clarissa
[wrote Lady Bradshaigh, who, when she had finished the first part, flung herself into correspondence under the pen-name of "Mrs. Belfour."] From
hints given in your four volumes, I have but too
much reason to apprehend a fatal catastrophe. . . .
Is it possible, that he who has the art to please in
softness, in the most natural, easy, humorous, and
sensible manner, can resolve to give joy only to the
ill-natured reader, and heave the compassionate
breast with tears for irremediable woes? Tears I
would choose to shed for virtue in distress; but still
would suffer to flow, in greater abundance, for unexpected turns of happiness, in which, Sir, you excel
any other author I ever read! When nature ought
to be touched, you make the very soul feel.

"Which consideration (amongst many others)
will, I hope, induce you not to vary from what has
given your good-natured and judicious readers so
much pleasure. It is not murder, or any other hor-
rid act, but the preceding distresses, which touch
and raise the passions of those, at least, whom an
author would wish to please, supposing him to be
such a one as I take you to be. Therefore, Sir, after
you have brought the divine Clarissa to the very
brink of destruction, let me intreat (may I say,
insist upon) a turn, that will make your almost
despairing readers half mad with joy. . . . "

But she admitted—"with a blush of the deepest

dye"—that for the life of her she couldn't help
liking Lovelace. "A sad dog! Why should you
make him so wicked, and yet so agreeable?"

Lovely, impetuous, ingenuous Lady Bradshaigh!
She rather underrated her charms in her letters to
Richardson, declaring that though she might write
"like a giddy girl of sixteen", she was "past the
romantic time of life." "I have common understanding and middling judgment, for one of my
sex, which I tell you for fear you should not find
it out; but if you take me for a fool, I do not care
a straw." Fortunately, a contemporary portrait of
her has been preserved—all that a woman should
be whose compassionate breast is heaved with tears
for irremediable woes.

The summer passed. The other three volumes
appeared. Remorseless Mr. Richardson dragged
Clarissa in the depths. "Excuse me, good Mr.
Richardson," wrote Lady Bradshaigh, "I cannot
go on; it is your fault—you have done more than
I can bear." She had "shed a pint of tears". Her
heart was "still bursting" as she wrote. Even her
otherwise invisible husband appeared on the scene,
"labouring through the sixth volume" and inter-
rupting her with transports of grief equal to her own.

After all, Lady Bradshaigh was only forty. But
Colley Cibber, old enough at seventy-seven to be
rather jaded, vied with Lady Bradshaigh. Cibber
and Richardson were friends. Richardson drew a
priceless picture of the two of them, together at

Tunbridge Wells, in that summer of '48. Colley
was paying court to the belle of the Wells, Elizabeth Chudleigh, who was to become Duchess of
Kingston and Countess of Bristol:

"She said pretty things [Richardson wrote]—
for she was Miss Chudleigh. He said pretty things
—for he was Mr. Cibber: and all the company, men
and women . . . . were half as well pleased as if they
had said the sprightly things themselves. . . . But
once I found the laureat squatted upon one of the
benches, with a face more wrinkled than ordinary
with disappointment. 'I thought,' said I, 'you were
of the party at the tea-treats—Miss Chudleigh is
gone into the tea-room.'—'Pshaw!' said he, 'there
is no coming at her, she is so surrounded by the
toupets.'—And I left him upon the fret.—But he
was called to soon after; and in he flew, and his
face shone again, and looked smooth. . . . "

"Lord, Lord! What figures do Mr. Nash and Mr.
Cibber make, hunting after new beauties, and with
faces of high importance traversing the walks!"
Richardson exclaims in a letter to Miss Highmore:

"God bless you, come and see them?—And if you
do, I will show you a still more grotesque figure
than either. A sly sinner, creeping along the very
edges of the walks, getting behind benches: one
hand in his bosom, the other held up to his chin, as
if to keep it in its place: afraid of being seen, as a
thief of detection. The people of fashion, if he hap-
pen to cross a walk (which he always does with
precipitation) *unsmiling* their faces, as if they

thought him in their way; and he as sensible of so being, stealing in and out of the book-seller's shop, as if he had one of their glass cases under his coat."

The friendship between the dashing old beau and the shy, class-conscious little printer is one of the quaintest things in the whole quaint story. Richardson could smile affectionately at Cibber's extravagances, but he could not bear to hear him criticized. Colley was the prize-joke of his time. His vanity was a joke, his Laureate Odes were a joke; as hero of the *Dunciad* he was an enshrined joke; but when Samuel Johnson described Colley's attempt to submit one of the Odes to him, and his stopping him with the exclamation that he "could not bear such nonsense", Richardson was vastly indignant that Johnson "did not treat Mr. Cibber with more respect."

Adept in the ways of Lovelaces, Colley could still feel with Clarissa. There is a kind of sardonic appropriateness in the fact that Richardson heard about it from Laetitia Pilkington. Laetitia was an out-at-elbows adventuress. In his kindly way, Richardson had helped her:

"I passed two hours this morning with Mr. Cibber [Laetitia wrote], whom I found in such real anxiety for Clarissa, as none but so perfect a master of nature could have excited. I had related to him, not only the catastrophe of the story, but also your truly religious and moral reason for it; and, when he heard what a dreadful lot her's was to be, he lost

all patience, threw down the book, and vowed he
would not read another line. To express or paint
his passion, would require such masterly hands as
yours, or his own: he shuddered; nay, the tears
stood in his eyes:—'What!' (said he), 'shall I, who
have loved and revered the virtuous, the beautiful
Clarissa, from the same motives I loved Mr. Richardson, bear to stand a patient spectator of her
ruin?' "

Much more there is, in Laetitia's letter, to the same
effect; and then:

"In this manner did the dear gentleman, I think
I may almost say, rave; for I never saw passion
higher wrought than his. When I told him she must
die, he said, 'G—d d—n him, if she should!' "

Adulation such as thus—albeit usually more
chastely phrased—Richardson battened on. He
surrounded himself with fervid women:

"I will tell you some of my haunts, if you please
[he wrote to Lady Bradshaigh]. I sometimes visit
Miss Westcomb, Ormond Street; sometimes Mrs.
Jodrell, in Bedford Row; sometimes Miss Highmore; sometimes the wife and sister (two very
agreeable women) of Mr. Millar, bookseller, in the
Strand. My acquaintance lies chiefly among the
ladies; I care not who knows it."

He read aloud to them, *currente calamo*, the most
moving passages from *Clarissa*. They flooded him
with sympathetic emotion. He had depicted a respectable maid-servant, whose virtue was richly re-

warded. He had depicted a noble virgin of the middle class, whose fate had heaved the compassionate breast with tears of irremediable woes. He had created a dashing blade, whom his fair readers, with blushes of the deepest dye, had found rather startlingly agreeable. Why shouldn't he, his adulators persuaded, depict a hero of the upper class, a male paragon? He swallowed the bait and wrote *Sir Charles Grandison.* Horace Walpole said that it was a picture of high life as conceived by a bookseller, and romance as it would be spiritualized by a Methodist teacher. Walpole was right, but the chorus of praise continued unabated. Richardson gave readings from *Sir Charles Grandison,* and distributed the sheets to his coterie. Mr. Cibber was as excited as he had been about *Clarissa:*

"I have just finished the sheets you favoured me with . . . Upon my soul I am so choked with suspense, that I won't tell you a word of the vast delight some had in Miss Byron's company, till you have repeated it by letting me see her again . . . Z-ds! I have not patience till I know what's become of her. . . . I will not give you a pretence to call me flatterer . . . yet since I was born I cannot say, that in all my reading of ancients and moderns, I ever met with such variety of entertainment, so much goodness of heart, and so indefatigable a capacity to give proofs of it. Can any man be a good moral writer that does not take up his pen in the cause of virtue? I had rather have the fame that your amiable zeal for it deserves, than be preferred as poet to a *Pope,* or his *Homer.*"

Are you tempted to discount these as mere Cibberian ravings? Listen then to Dr. Benjamin Kennicott, Fellow of Exeter; Whitehall preacher; Fellow of the Royal Society; Radcliffe Librarian; canon of Christ Church, Oxford; editor of the *Vetus Testamentum Hebraicum, cum variis lectionibus:*

"You will not, you cannot, think me insincere; because every man, you know, makes his own character with Sir Charles Grandison, and is always believed good till found otherwise. . . . I must assure you that I know not the man upon earth I more honour, as the true friend, and (which completes the character) the successful friend, of virtue. And not a little vanity, of course, possesses me, at having leave to call the friend of mankind, *my* friend."

"The friend of mankind." Were not the French reading *Sir Charles Grandison* in the translation of Abbé Prévost, who had previously regaled them with translations of *Pamela* and *Clarissa*? Were not the Germans reading "a translation of *Clarissa* in eight volumes, from the celebrated Dr. Haller, Vice-Chancellor of the University of Göttengen"? Were not the Dutch reading a translation of *Clarissa* "by an eminent hand, M. Stinstra, of Haarlingen"? Had not the celebrated Italian dramatist, Carlo Goldoni, "done" *Pamela* into two comedies, *Pamela Nubile* and *Pamela Maritata,* performed in thronged Venetian theatres?

Praise from the ladies; praise from men of

fashion; praise from the learned; praise from the European world. What more could there conceivably be? A pedestal? A shrine? Well, at least a grotto.

Grottos were the vogue. Pope had started it with his grotto at Twickenham. Flatterers gathered there to pay court to the famous poet. Pope derided them:

"What walls can guard me, or what shades can
    hide?
They pierce my thickets, through my grot they
    glide. . . .
Is there a parson, much bemused in beer,
A maudlin poetess, a rhyming peer,
A clerk, foredoomed his father's soul to cross,
Who pens a stanza when he should engross? . . .
All fly to Twitenham—"

Richardson welcomed them. He built his grotto in the garden back of the stately house at North End near Hammersmith, which he bought when he was at the height of his prosperity. There his coterie gathered. Dr. Johnson said that Richardson could talk of nothing but his own books, but the coterie asked nothing better. Colley Cibber, with his "female fry" as the gallant old gentleman called them; Hester Mulso, precocious authoress of *The Loves of Amoret and Melissa* and *The Story of Fidelia*: who, after rejecting Gilbert White of Selborne, married "a sensible, ingenious, modest young gentleman", John Chapone, and, as "the celebrated

Mrs. Chapone," wrote *Letters on the Improvement of the Mind*; Mrs. Delany, one of the "Blues," whose six volumes of *Autobiography and Correspondence* are entertaining records of the social life of the time; Susannah Highmore, daughter of the portrait-painter who drew the illustrations for the first editions of *Pamela* and *Clarissa,* and herself an artist of no mean ability—these and sundry others gathered in the grotto to argue—sweetly— with Mr. Richardson about the doings of Pamela and Mr. B——, Clarissa and Lovelace, Sir Charles and Clementina and Harriet Byron—and to listen to his ever-ready readings.

They were tearful gatherings. His admirers could not read him aloud to one another:

"What must have been your feelings [said Miss Highmore] at the time you wrote what nobody can read without streaming eyes and heart-breaking sorrow? It has had the same effect on my mother and father as on myself. We could none of us read aloud the affecting scenes we met with, but each read to ourselves, and in separate apartments wept."

But with Mr. Richardson himself reading the affecting scenes—and by now he did it dry-eyed— his auditors could luxuriate in grief.

It was probably because handkerchiefs would have concealed the countenance that Miss Highmore did not so depict his auditors in the drawing which she made of one of these readings. But it is a spirited drawing. Within the narrow confines of the grotto, on the extreme left, sits round little Mr. Richardson, in velvet cap and morning gown, his right hand characteristically "in his bosom," his left hand holding the manuscript of *Sir Charles Grandison*. Next him, with faces intently turned, are Hester Mulso's father and brother; opposite, grouped round a table, are Miss Prescott, who was to marry Hester's brother; the fair artist, Miss Highmore; and, centred in the open doorway with its vista of garden foliage, Hester Mulso. At the extreme right, somewhat too nonchalantly taking snuff, is Mr. Duncombe, Miss Highmore's lover. But it is evident that Mr. Richardson is just beginning one of the affecting scenes. Mr. Mulso, senior, is already reaching for his handkerchief.

And to the grotto came pilgrims from abroad. Herr Reich of Leipsig:

"set out for London purely with a view of cultivating a personal acquaintance with so great a man as Mr. Samuel Richardson. . . . After chocolate, Mr. Richardson brought us into the garden. . . . Everything I saw, everything I tasted, recalled to me the idea of the golden age . . In the middle of the garden, over against the house, we came to a kind of grotto. . . . It was on this seat, Mr. LeFevre (Mr. Richardson's friend) told me, that Pamela, Clarissa, and Grandison received their birth; I kissed the ink-horn on the side of it. . . . In the evening, I took my leave of the family and returned with Mr. Richardson. I saw him several times since, during the eight days I staid in England; but it was necessary, at last, to quit that divine man. . . . He embraced me, and a mutual tenderness deprived us of speech. He accompanied me with his eyes as far as he could: I shed tears."

Mr. Richardson had arrived. *Sir Charles Grandison* was published in 1753. He had nine years more in which to enjoy it. Let Dr. Johnson write *finis*: "That fellow died merely from want of change among his flatterers. He perished for want of *more*, like a man obliged to breathe the same air till it is exhausted."

OFFICIAL POETS

THE court-poet, officially recognized and re-warded, belongs to an old tradition. Demodocus "takes up the tale" of the Trojan war to entertain the visiting Odysseus. Hrothgar's scôp takes up the tale of the Finn Saga to entertain the visiting Beowulf. A less generally known example is the visit of the King's Poet, Gunlaug Snakestongue, to England, as related in the *Corpus Poeticum Boreale*:

"Gunlaug, setting sail from Norway, where he had got into some trouble by his bold tongue and ready hand, came to London Bridge and found King Aethelred Eadgarsson ruling in England. He goes before the king who asks him whence he came and who he was. Gunlaug answers and adds: 'And I have come to see *you*, my lord, because I have made a poem about you and I should like you to listen to it.' The king said that he would, and Gunlaug delivered his poem boldly. The king thanks him and gives him a scarlet cloak lined with the finest fur, and laced down the skirt, for his poet's fee. He then goes to Dublin. At that time King Sigtrygg Silkbeard . . . was ruling over Ireland, and he had been ruling but a short while. He received the poet well, and Gunlaug said, 'I have made a poem on you, and I should like to have silence.' The King answered, 'No man before up to this time has done this and brought me a poem.

Thou shalt surely be heard.' Then he delivered his song of praise. The King thanked him for his poem, and called to his treasurer, saying, 'How shall this poem be repaid?' 'How do you wish to repay it, my lord?' answered he. 'How will it be paid,' says the king, 'if I give him two ships of burden?' 'That is too much, my lord,' says he; 'other kings give goodly gifts as poets' fees—good swords, or good gold rings.' The King gave him his coat of new scarlet, a laced kirtle, a cloak of noble fur, and a gold ring of great price."

The caution of this King's Treasurer is itself the beginning of a tradition—the tightening of the official purse-strings against that most anomalous of beings, the man who does nothing in the world more important than making verses. When Sir Walter Raleigh, bringing with him the first three books of the *Faerie Queene,* appealed to Elizabeth on Spenser's behalf, Her Majesty, so the story goes, "ordered a goodly sum to be awarded to the newe poete. . . . The penurious Lord Treasurer . . . demurred, dropping *sotto voce* the question, 'What? All this for a song?' "

When the Normans entered England, Duke William's advancing host were led by a court minstrel, singing of Charlemagne and Roland and Oliver and their vassals who died at Roncesvalles— a minstrel who asked as his reward only that he might be permitted to strike the first blow in the battle. The minstrels in the households of the Norman barons, King's poets of their little principalities, sang to their masters, as the author of the

Cursor Mundi tells us, stories of Alexander the Great, of Julius Caesar, of the siege of Troy, of King Arthur, of Charlemagne and Roland, of Tristram and Yseult—

> "Of pryncis, prelates and of kinges,
> Songis sere of selcouth rime
> As English, Frankis and Latine."

In spite of the penuriousness of treasurers, these court entertainers often received rich gifts from their baron or their king. William the Conqueror gave estates in Gloucestershire to his *joculator regis*. Everyone knows of Henry I's court entertainer, Rahere, who "in contrition for an ill-spent life," founded, in 1123, the Hospital and Priory of St. Bartholomew in Smithfield.

Upon the accession of Henry II, the King's court became a centre of literary activity—even of classical culture. In this "paradise of clerks" as it was called, Roger of Hoveden, Gervase of Tilbury, Ralph de Diceto, Richard of Devizes, John of Salisbury, William of Newburgh, Giraldus Cambrensis, Walter Map, Joseph of Exeter, Geoffrey of Vinsauf, are notable figures. The arts became respectable. The King's entertainer, who had in former times been hardly more than a court jester, rose in the social scale. The marriage of Henry to Eleanor of Aquitaine, granddaughter of William IX, Count of Poitiers, one of the most famous of aristocratic troubadours, brought into the English court a form of minstrelsy peculiarly identified with courtly

usage. Eleanor's troubadour lover, Bernard de
Ventadour, is said to have joined his mistress in
England. Eleanor's countryman, Bertran de Born,
count and troubadour, was the chief thorn in
Henry's side in Aquitaine. In an old Provençal
sketch of Bertran, quoted by Miss Norgate, in her
England under the Angevin Kings, it is said:

"He was a good knight and a good warrior, and
a good servant of ladies, and a good troubadour of
sirventes . . . and whenever he chose, he was
master of King Henry and his sons; but he always
wanted them to be at war among themselves, the
father and the sons and the brothers one with another; and he always wanted the King of France
and King Henry to be at war too. And if they made
peace or a truce, he immediately set to work to
unmake it with his *sirventes,* and to show how they
were all dishonoured in peace. And he gained much
good by it, and much harm."

This troubadour influence tended to dignify the
rôle of the court-poet. With the accession of King
Richard, the English court became a veritable court
of troubadours. Around him clustered Arnaut
Daniel, Peire Vidal, Folquet of Marseilles, Gaucelm
Faidit. The troubadour Ambroise sang at his
coronation. And every reader of Scott's *Talisman*
will remember the more or less mythical Blondel,
who discovered his imprisoned master.

Henry III's marriage with Eleanor of Provence
continued the troubadour connection. In Henry
III's reign, the title of *versificator regis* appears for

the first time in the king's household. The holder
of the title, Henri d'Avranches, was no mere professional minstrel. His Latin poems are quoted by
the historian Matthew Paris. The Exchequer rolls
record various substantial gifts to Magistro
Henrico, Versificatori, and also a life-time grant of
wine.

"To Master Henry de Abrincis, the King's Poet,
two tuns of wine of the King's wines, which are in
the keeping of the Chamberlain of London, to wit,
a tun of vintage and a tun of sack."

We all know that when the Laureateship was finally
established in the seventeenth century, a grant of
wine was one of the perquisites of the office, and
remained so till 1790 when Henry James Pye com-
pounded it for cash. Southey who succeeded Pye,
wrote to Walter Scott: "The butt of sack is now
wickedly commuted to £26."

Scott replied:

"Is there no way of getting rid of that iniquitous
Modus, and requiring the *butt* in kind? I would
have you think of it; I know no man so well entitled
to Xeres' sack as yourself, though many bards
would make a better figure at drinking it. I should
think that in due time a memorial might get some
relief in this part of the appointment—it should be
at least £100 wet and £100 dry. When you have
carried your point of discarding the ode and my
point of getting the sack, you will be exactly in the
situation of Davy in the farce, who stipulated for

more wages, less work, and the key to the ale-
cellar."

When I was at Oxford in 1919 tracing the history
of the Laureateship, Mr. Bridges confessed to me
that he had never known why part of his laureateship fee, or honorarium, or whatever it ought to be
called, came from the Lord Chamberlain's department and another part from the Lord Steward's.
The books of the Lord Chamberlain's department
show an annual payment to the poet-laureate of
£72, and upon the accounts of the Lord Steward's
department is still recorded an annual payment to
the poet-laureate of £27 "in lieu of a butt of sack".

I do not know whether the Olympians ever con-
sult Bacchus in these modern days, but it has
always seemed to me that Mr. Henry James Pye
must have much to answer for.

Master Henry de Abrincis' two tuns have led us
far afield. Let us get back to the beginnings. After
the reign of Henry III, the title of *versificator regis*
drops out of the records. Meanwhile the word
laureatus begins to make its way into common use
by way of the universities. In the University of
Paris, the Degree of Master of Arts conferred the
right to teach. Until he obtained that degree the
student was a *baccalarius artium* or bachelor of
arts. But, apparently in the thirteenth century, it
became customary to confirm this preliminary
status by an unofficial, or quasi-official ceremony,
conducted not by the chancellor or faculty but by

the "Nation" to which the student belonged. The word *baccalarius* has no etymological connection with the laurel of classical tradition. The *Oxford Dictionary* derives it tentatively from Low Latin *bacca* (*vacca*), a cow, *baccalis*, a grazing farm, *baccalarius*, cow-boy or graziers' apprentice, hence any youth in service. The unpledged knight, like the "yong Squyer" of the *Canterbury Tales*, was a *bacheler*. But the resemblance of *baccalarius* to the traditional symbol of poetical fame was too close to be overlooked. In the statutes of the University of Paris, the degree, or status, seems to have been explicitly referred to as the *laurea baccalaureus*. The recipients had crowns of laurel placed upon their heads and styled themselves "laureates". With the establishment in the thirteenth century of the first three Oxford Colleges, the word "laureate" begins to be used, in this academic sense, in England. The association of the *baccalarius* with the laurel was taken for granted. Says quaint old John Ayliffe in his *Antient and Present State of Oxford* (1714):

"In laurel, those small *pillulae* we call *bacchae*, which this tree buds forth as flowers. And because there is hope for the flower, this term *Baccha Lauri* is given to young students in hopes they will afterwards merit the laurel crown."

There is a detailed description of this academic crowning with laurel in Anthony Wood's *History and Antiquities of the University of Oxford*. Wood says that Robert Whitinton, a famous grammarian in the reign of Henry VIII, was one of the last to be so crowned. Whitinton's "laureation" occurred in 1512.

I have dwelt on this academic usage of the word "laureate" partly because it first gave vogue in England to the title Poet Laureate, and partly because it accounts for misunderstandings among those who have interested themselves in the traditions of the laureateship. Robert Baston, for example, who flourished in the late thirteenth and early fourteenth centuries, is described by both Bale and Anthony Wood as a poet laureate of Oxford; but Warton in his *History of English Poetry* and various writers about the laureateship since his day have without a shadow of warrant described him as "Poet Laureate to Edward II". In like manner, writers about the laureateship, to say nothing of biographers of the poet, persist in describing John Skelton as "Poet Laureate to Henry VIII", though Skelton himself makes it perfectly clear that his laureateship was an academic distinction:

> "At Oxforth, the universyte,
> Avaunsid I was to that degre;
> By hole consent of theyr senate,
> I was made poete laureate."

Among these academic poets laureate, it happens, however, that there is one who did receive an annuity from the King and is designated in the letters patent conferring the annuity, as "Poet Laureate".

This was the blind poet, Bernard Andreas, who after the manner of later laureates, wrote sundry fulsome eulogies of Henry VIII, some in Latin, some in French, and who, as it happens, was also Historiographer-Royal. This is interesting because the appointment of the first of the present succession of Poets Laureate, John Dryden, conjoined the post of Historiographer-Royal with the laureateship.

It does not seem worth while here to make more than passing reference to the fact that Chaucer and Spenser have been sometimes numbered among the poets laureate. Everyone knows that the annuity of twenty marks and the supplementary grant of a daily pitcher of wine which Chaucer received from Edward III were for services other than poetic, and that grants of wine were also made to other members of the King's household. As for the fifty pounds for Edmund Spenser, which Raleigh's intercession won from the grudging Burghley, it seems to have carried nothing with it. References not only to Chaucer and Spenser, but also to Daniel and Drayton, as poets laureate occur in poetical tributes to them, but only as a convention of eulogy.

For laying the foundations of the present laureateship, we must thank Ben Jonson. They were only foundations. There is absolutely no warrant for naming him the first of the present succession. For his services to the Court, particularly as a writer of masques, he received two grants of pen-

sion, the first, of one hundred marks, in 1616; the
second, in 1630, increasing the amount to £100
and adding a "terse of Canary Spanish Wyne
yearly". They carried no title or official recognition. But Ben, conscious of his importance as pro-
ducer of the annual masque, liked to proclaim himself "King's Poet". In his *Masque of Augurs,*
Jonson and Inigo Jones are referred to as "King's
Poet" and "King's Architect", and in the dialogue
between the Poet and the Cook, in *Neptune's
Triumph,* the Poet says:

"The most unprofitable of his servants I, sir—
the Poet. A kind of Christmas Ingine; one that is
used, at least once a year, for a trifling instrument
of wit or so."

It would appear that Ben, with his learning and
antiquarian tastes, induced the learned Selden to
include in his second and greatly enlarged edition
of *Titles of Honours* a disquisition on the title *Poet
Laureate*—a disquisition which Selden concludes
with the statement that he has thus "performed a
promise to you, my beloved Ben Jonson." Selden
discourses at length on the classical tradition; the
crowning of Petrarch with a wreath of laurels on
the Capitoline; and the practice of the German
Counts Palatine of giving the crown of laurel to
poets. Of this last, he cites several examples and
describes the ceremonial in detail. I am inclined to
think that Ben engineered this as a broad hint on

his own behalf. Nothing came of it—officially; but
this reminder of an ancient custom, given with all
the weight of Selden's authority, was not without
effect. Jonson's contempories fell into the habit of
complimenting him with the title. And posterity
has followed their example. Dear, arrogant old
Ben! It would have pleased him to know that his-
torians of literature were to name him as the first
of the official succession of poets laureate.

Sir William Davenant is usually listed as the
second of the "official" laureates; but there is no
reason to believe that his status differed from Jonson's. Like Jonson, Davenant wrote masques for
the Court. In 1638, Davenant, with Inigo Jones'
assistance, produced *Britannia Triumphans,* the
most gorgeous masque on record. The royal patent
of Dec. 13th, 1638, granting "William Davenant,
Gentleman", a pension of one hundred pounds "in
consideration of service heretofore done and here-
after to be done", is for his masques. In this sense
he was, if you like, King's Poet, just as Jonson had
been. I may be accused of attaching too much importance to a mere form of words. But it is true, is
it not, that the title poet laureate, conferred by the
Crown, does, with all the connotations with which
tradition has enriched it, single a poet out from his
fellow-poets as *the* poet whom the King delights to
honour? In Jonson's time and in Davenant's, the
inclination thus to single out a poet had not manifested itself. Jonson and Davenant are simply pen-

sioned for their services, "heretofore done and here-
after to be done", as suppliers of court masques.

But, unofficially, the idea of thus setting one
poet apart from the rest was taking shape. Though
no edition of Davenant's plays, masques or poems,
published during his life time, affixes the title to
his name, his friends did not hesitate so to refer to
him. Aubrey assumes that Jonson held the office,
and that Davenant was his official successor—
"After Ben Jonson's death," he says, "Davenant
was made laureate." At the Restoration Davenant
was prompt to reassert his claim to recognition as
court poet. His *Poem upon His Sacred Majesty's
Most Happy Return to His Dominions* was quickly
supplemented by an equally long and equally fulsome *Poem to the King's Most Sacred Majesty.*
Nothing came of them. Examination of the Pells
Issue Books from 1660 to 1668 indicates that
Charles II did not even renew the pension granted
by Charles I. The *Calendar of State Papers* for
1661 contains four references to Davenant in connection with theatre licences, but none in any other
connection. And though the same volume contains
references to one hundred and forty-two officers of
the King's household, there is no mention of a
"King's poet" or "poet laureate". But the title
which had been for so long unofficially accorded to
Davenant, the court did ultimately, if somewhat
belatedly, recognize and sanction; for six days after
Davenant's death a warrant was issued:

"For a grant to John Dryden of the Office of Poet Laureate, void by the death of Sir William Davenant."

This warrant of 1668, and the letters patent of August 18, 1670, appointing John Dryden, for his "many good and acceptable services" and on account of his "learninge and eminent abilityes . . . our Poett Laureatt and Historiographer Royall" are, I believe, the first official documents appointing a Poet Laureate. Henry VIII's grant of an annuity to Bernard Andreas does not constitute a precedent. For that document makes it clear that Bernard was already possessed of the title, and implies that he had had it from Oxford.

With John Dryden, then, the official succession of laureates, continuous to the present time, begins. He held the honour for twenty years, under two kings. He gave the laureateship a peculiar significance. No laureate since his day has used the office as Dryden used it. It is true that he wrote a few panegyrics. *Threnodia Augustalis,* "a funeral-Pindaric poem, sacred to the happy memory of King Charles II," and *Britannia Rediviva,* "a poem on the Prince, born on the Tenth of June, 1688," are in what we have come to think the conventional laureate vein. But in the main, he conceived himself as the officially sanctioned spokesman of the King in problems of state. The laureate's poetic genius and his unequalled satirical power were at the service, in turn, of each of his royal masters. *Absalom and*

Achitophel, The Medal, Religio Laici, and *The Hind and the Panther* are thus to be understood. How interesting it would have been if Dryden's successors, instead of contenting themselves with the manufacture of birthday Odes, had had the genius and the daring thus to fight for causes! It is at least a subject for speculation. What might have happened, for example, if William Congreve, with his rare and varied powers, had succeeded to the laureateship and had ventured to carry on, in Dryden's vein? We may recall Dryden's lines *To My Dear Friend, Mr. Congreve*:

> "O that your Brows my Lawrel had sustain'd,
> Well had I been depos'd, if you had reign'd!
> The Father had descended for the Son,
> For only You are lineal to the Throne."

But in 1689, when Dryden was deposed, Congreve was an unknown youth of eighteen, and the laurel passed to Shadwell:

> "Mature in dullness from his tender years."

The Earl of Dorset is quoted as saying when asked why he had not chosen a better poet:

> "I will not pretend to determine how great a poet Shadwell may be, but I am sure he is an honest man."

That was to be the basis of selection for more than a century following.

It is not necessary to burden this essay with an enumeration of Shadwell's successors. The attributes and peculiarities of the office are of greater interest than the lives, and the portentous effusions, of the men who held it. Upon Shadwell's death, the post of Historiographer-Royal became separated from the Laureateship. The Laureateship went to Nahum Tate, the office of Historiographer to Thomas Rymer. They have not since been joined, though when the Historiographer, Louis Dutens, died in 1812, Southey, then Poet Laureate, sought to obtain the appointment and renew the traditional union. As Poet Laureate and Historiographer, Dryden and Shadwell received £300. Nahum Tate's emolument from the laureateship alone was £100. At that figure it has remained ever since. Even when Henry James Pye petitioned to have the butt of sack commuted for cash, the careful George *included* the estimated value, £26, in the £100 instead of *adding* it to that amount!

From Dryden's day on, through the eighteenth century, the Poet Laureate appears in the records among the "King's officers and Servants in Ordinary above Stairs under the Lord Chamberlain." This specific inclusion of the Poet Laureate among the "King's Officers and Servants" raises the interesting question of the traditional "duties" of the office. In the days of Dryden, Shadwell and Tate, no duties were specified. From choice rather than necessity, Dryden, as we have seen, acted as spokes-

man and poet-advocate for the King. Shadwell
and Tate went their lumbering way, producing
occasional odes and panegyrics. It was under the
first George, upon the accession of Nicholas Rowe
to the laureateship, that the annual production of a
New Year's Ode and a *Birthday Ode* became the
Laureate's recognized duty. These *Odes* were sung
in the Chapel Royal, the orchestration being supplied by the "King's Band of Music". Is it any
wonder that the words were dull? Says Pope, in
his footnote to his satirical reference in the *Dunciad*
to Colley Cibber's New Year *Odes*:

"Made by the Poet Laureate for the time being,
to be sung at Court on every New Year's Day, the
words of which are happily drowned in the instru-
ments."

Says Whitehead in his *Pathetic Apology for all
Laureates, Past, Present and to Come*:

"His Muse, obliged by sack and pension,
    Without a subject or invention,
    Must certain words in order set
    As innocent as a Gazette. . . . .
    Content with Boyce's harmony,
    Who throws on many a worthless lay
    His music and his powers away."

These New Year and Birthday *Odes* came from
the hard-pushed pens of the successive laureates,
with unbroken regularity, throughout the rest of

the eighteenth century. Not until 1813 was a protest heard. Henry James Pye died. The Lord
Chamberlain, Lord Hertford, offered the laureateship to Walter Scott. Scott refused. Southey, albeit somewhat piqued at being second choice, accepted. To Croker Southey had written:

"I would not write odes as boys write exercises,
at stated times and upon stated subjects; but if it
were understood that upon great public events I
might either write or be silent as the spirit moved,
I should now accept the office, as an honourable
distinction, which under those circumstances it
would become."

Southey had understood Croker to promise that he
should be relieved of the annual duty. But on the
approach of the second New Year's Day Southey
found himself compelled to continue. The annual
New Year *Odes* were required of the Laureate
throughout the Regency; and when the old King
died and George IV came at last to the throne,
Mr. Shields, Master of the King's Music, wrote to
Southey:

"Our most gracious and royal master intends to
command the performance of an Ode at St. James'
on the day fixed for the celebration of his birthday."

But during the several months delay before the
Coronation, wiser counsels prevailed. The *Ode*
which Southey prepared was not performed. The

old custom lapsed, and happily, has not since been renewed. But though Southey had accepted the laureateship under the impression that upon great public events he "might either write or be silent as the spirit moved", and though he held it for more than twenty years after his exemption from the annual *Odes,* the office never ceased to spur him.

"The Laureateship will certainly have this effect upon me [he had written to Neville White in 1814] that it will make me produce more poetry than I otherwise should have done."

No one who reads doggedly through the many volumes of Southey's poetical works, can refrain from echoing Byron's exclamation:

"O Southey! Southey! cease thy varied song!
A bard may chaunt too often and too long."

Southey is an example of one of the perils of the laureateship. Unless the laureate have the fine obstinacy of a Robert Bridges, or the craftsman's conscience of a Tennyson, he is altogether too likely to write because he is laureate whether the spirit moves him or not. The effusions of Bridges' predecessor, Alfred Austin, are a warning.

Between Southey's death and our own day, the course of the laureateship is a twice-told tale. The conferring of it upon Wordsworth in his old age was recognition pure and simple. "I will undertake that you shall have nothing required from you," wrote Sir Robert Peel. The nation honoured itself in honouring him. Tennyson gave to the office a distinction which it had not had since Dryden's day, and a new significance. For forty-two years he was the voice of England, the celebrant of her beauties, the interpreter of her moods. That the appointment of a successor to Tennyson should result in an anticlimax was almost inevitable. Swinburne was available; but Queen Victoria's austerely remote "*I am told* that Mr. Swinburne is the best poet in my dominions," and Gladstone's reply that "the turbulency of Swinburne's political opinions make it impossible even to consider his claims to the laurel" put an end to that. William Morris, George Meredith, Coventry Patmore, Austin Dobson, William Watson were available. Gladstone waited, and went out of office without having made an appointment. Lord Rosebery came, and went, without making an appointment. Four years passed, during which the laureateship dropped out of the public mind and was like to die a natural death. And then Lord Salisbury appointed Alfred Austin.

Let us not talk about that. We can still, if we like, dig up from contemporary newspapers Austin's initial fiasco, the poem entitled *Jameson's Ride*; but we shall not find that poem in Alfred Austin's *Collected Poems*. Austin remained laureate for seventeen years. When he died in 1913, Mr. Kip-

ling's star had risen. Austin Dobson and William
Watson were left from the earlier group. Messrs.
Newbolt, Noyes, Yeats, Masefield, Stephen Phil-
lips, Housman, had come to the fore. Thomas
Hardy, quietly and unconcernedly pursuing his own
way, was becoming more and more widely known.
But Mr. Asquith, Prime Minister and man of let-
ters, appointed Robert Bridges.

This is not the place, and indeed there is no
necessity, for me to undertake a critical discussion
of Bridges' poetry. Aside from his distinction as a
poet, it must now be recognized—despite a little
silly talk to the contrary—that Bridges played a
distinguished part as England's Poet Laureate. He
went his own way. He was what Southey meant to
be, but was not—silent upon public events unless
the spirit moved. I know from Bridges himself that
he was not indifferent to the honour which the
nation conferred upon him in 1913; and every
reader of the volume entitled *October and Other
Poems with Occasional Verses on the War* must be
aware how responsive he really was to the nobler
and finer moods of that era of confusion. But he
could be wisely silent.

"Amid the flimsy joys of the uproarious city
  my spirit on those first jubilant days of armistice
 was heavier within me, and felt a profounder fear
 than ever it knew in all the War's darkest dismay."

(*The Testament of Beauty*)

Opinion is divided as to whether *The Testament of Beauty* is a great poem or not. I shall content myself with pointing out that the poem creates an interesting precedent in the laureate tradition. The King singles out one poet from the rest by naming him the poet of the nation, the Poet Laureate. For sixteen years—from 1913 to 1929—the Laureate responded occasionally to national impulses and moods, but on the whole followed his own rather esoteric bent as an experimenter with unusual and not very widely appreciated metres. And then, as his life drew to a close, he put all of himself—his mature wisdom, his philosophy of beauty and his subtle art—into a single long poem, which he published as Poet Laureate and dedicated to the King. That is one way, and I am inclined to think a very good way, for a Poet Laureate to respond to the honour which the nation has paid him.

* * * *

Here again (1935), a postscript. Mr. John Masefield, the present poet laureate, shot his bolt twenty years ago. The bolt was good while it lasted, but it did not last. The effect upon him of his appointment to the laureateship has been what it was upon Southey—that it has made him "produce more poetry than he otherwise should have done." Unfortunate, isn't it, that with a few precious exceptions, the appointment stimulates the bard to "chaunt too often and too long"? Well, we have our ups and downs.

III

AN OLD BOOK SHELF

I T SEEMS but yesterday—or this night, rather. And as this night I shall describe it—though I should hate to admit how many years ago it was. The *mise en scène* is the "Dark Room". The Dark Room is a spacious apartment which, through some inexplicable aberration of the architect, was dropped, windowless, transomeless, almost airless, in the blind centre of the whimsical old house in which I spent my boyhood. The Dark Room is too large to be called a closet, and too maimed to be used for anything else. And so it is given over to the outworn miscellanies of many generations.

At one end of the Dark Room is the book shelf, or rather a row of them—a book closet, the veritable altar of Oblivion. It must have been my great grandmother who laid the first obsolescent volume upon the lowest shelf of the bare closet. And ever since, through the successive generations, other books have followed it until they began to crowd each other and climb, level by level, toward the top. Finally, perhaps, when my great-grandmother's granddaughter was a girl in her teens, the books reached the top shelf, which projects up behind the wall; and there they gathered one by one in a silent company with their toes visibly on the shelf

169

and their heads invisibly erected into the nook of the wall. There they gathered until the already crowded neighbours were pushed aside to receive one more thin little volume—and then the closet doors were shut, and the Dark Room door was shut, and the denizens of the book closet settled themselves to sober contemplation.

It was twenty years ago, perhaps, when that last volume was crowded in upon its fellows; and twenty more years might have spread their dust upon them, had it not been that the Fates cut the thread of the good old house. Progress steps unfamiliarly through the wide halls, judges the dreamy silence with critical disapproval, and decides to sell. And leave those volumes to the curious eye of the stranger? No, that at least must not be. We will look over the book closet to-night.

And nightfall finds us—the two Aunties and me —peering by the dim light of a candle along the dusty shelves. I am only I, and there's an end. The two Aunties are the only ones who make any difference. They are young ladies of sixty-five or thereabouts. Aunt Ruth is perhaps a year or two younger than Aunt Rachel, but they have been young together for so many years that that, too, doesn't count. Aunt Rachel is tall and slender and white-haired and brown-eyed. She has a slight imperfection in her lower lip—due to a cut, from a fall in her childhood, I have been told—which gives her a queer crooked little smile when she is merry. She never laughs aloud; but she is often merry, and that slow, crooked little smile is one of the most persuasive things that I have ever seen. She has a delicate and very fragrant humour, has Aunt Rachel, and though just forty summers ago she ceased to grow any older, she has adjusted herself to the changing moods of the world during these last two score years. Aunt Ruth, too, is tall and slender and white-haired and brown-eyed. Her face is fairer in its symmetry than Aunt Rachel's but she is less often merry. She is not so adaptive as her sister. There is a touch of melancholy in her mood, and she lives in the Past—the Past of the 1860's and '70's, when the young men came to woo,—and wooed in vain, for the sisters found the love of no man potent enough to separate them the one from the other.

It is in this Past that we are to-night,—a Past that comes dimly back to life again as we look over these books that Aunt Ruth and Aunt Rachel had read and laid aside fifty, forty, thirty, twenty years ago.

Aunt Rachel falls to counting with a merry smile. "One, two, three copies of *Charlotte Temple —Love and Romance,* by Susannah Rowson. And the motto

'She was her parents' only joy.
They had but one, one darling child.'

How we did enjoy reading that love-sick tale! And

how we sympathized with Charlotte! And how instructive and elevating to youth and innocence that story was supposed to be! And that reminds me. Do you remember, Ruth, the books of instruction to young girls, which we were fed on in our teens and early twenties? They must be tucked away somewhere in this closet. Yes, here they are."

And she gathers from here and there on the shelves a series of worn little volumes in faded cloth bindings and lays them before me. I read their titles aloud: *The Young Woman's Guide to Excellence, by William A. Alcott, Author of The Young Man's Guide, Young Husband, Young Wife, Young Mother, etc., etc., Thirteenth Edition, Boston, 1847.* ("Professor of things in general," I remark irreverently. "Wonder what the *and-so-forths* stood for." But Aunt Ruth frowns and I read on): *Letters to a Young Lady on a Variety of Useful and Interesting Subjects, Calculated to Improve the Heart, to Form the Manners and Enlighten the Understanding, by the Rev. John Bennett. Tenth American Edition, Philadelphia, 1856. The Young Maiden, by A. B. Muzzey, Author of The Young Man's Friend, Boston, 1840. A Woman's Thoughts about Women, by the Author of John Halifax, Gentleman, New York, 1858.*

"Now that last," breaks in Aunt Rachel, with decision, "was a good sensible book; but those others! Their authors treated us as if our bodies had the growth of twenty years and our minds were still in swaddling clothes."

"Yes," adds Aunt Ruth, "and they planned our love affairs for us,—as if a young girl dreamed her most romantic dreams by rote, and learned how to say yes or no out of the catechism!"

"Now, just look at this," says Aunt Rachel, and she turns to *The Young Woman's Guide*:

" 'Once, at least, in twenty-four hours, the whole surface of the body should be washed in soap and water, and receive the friction of a coarse towel. This may be done by warm or cold bathing; by a plunging or shower bath; by means of a common wash-tub; and even without further preparation than an ordinary wash-bowl and sponge.

" 'By washing a small part of the person at a time, rubbing it well, and then covering what is done, the whole may be washed in cold water, even in winter time.

" 'Would that our daughters and sisters—the daughters and sisters of America, especially, were so far apprized of this indispensable requisite, as to need no monitor on the subject! But, unhappily it is not so. Very far from it, on the contrary.' "

"Now *what*, Ned, in your modern college slang, —now *what* did Mr. William A. Alcott take us for?"

"But this same gentleman's theology was as doubtful as his hygiene was obvious. See how he puts it. Beauty, he says, is a virtue. 'There can hardly be a doubt that Adam and Eve were exceedingly beautiful; nor that so far as the world can

be restored to its primitive state—which we hope
may be the case in its future glorious ages—the
pristine beauty of our race will be restored. . . .
In falling, with our first parents, we fell physically
as well as morally; and our physical departure
from truth is almost as wide as our moral. I suppose all the ugliness of the young' (I am afraid Mr.
Alcott didn't like children) 'comes directly or in-
directly from the transgression of God's laws,
natural or moral; and can only be restored by
obedience to those laws, by the transgression of
which it came.' "

"But, my dear," protests Aunt Ruth, "the Bible
says that Adam and Eve were beautiful; and Mr.
Alcott was considered a great authority in his day."

Aunt Rachel's question goes unanswered and she
picks up the *Letters to Young Ladies*. "Time was,"
says Aunt Rachel, as she turns the leaves of the
little volume, "when we thought that the sum of all
wisdom was contained between these covers. There
are just one hundred and thirteen letters to 'My
dear Lucy,' and they deal, as the Rev. Mr. Bennett
explains in the preface, with:

I. Religious Knowledge, with a list of proper
writers.

II. Polite Knowledge, as it relates to the *Belles
Lettres* in general: Epistolary Writing, History,
the Lives of Particular Persons, Geography, Natural History, Astronomy, Poetry, Sculpture, Archi-
tecture, Heraldry, Voyages, Travels, and so forth;
with a catalogue of, and criticisms upon the most
approved authors under each article.

III. Accomplishments, as displayed in Needle-work, Embroidery, Drawing, Music, Dancing, Dress, Politeness, and so forth.

IV. Prudential Conduct and Maxims, with respect to Amusements, Love, Courtship, Marriage, and so forth!

"It must have been at least forty-five years since I drank at this fountain of knowledge. I wonder how it would appeal to me to-day." And she runs her eye over the pages.

"What do you think of this, Ned, with your co-educational colleges and your *new women?*

" 'The prominent excellencies of *your* minds are taste and imagination, and your knowledge should be of a kind which assimilates with these faculties. Politics, Philosophy, Mathematics, or Metaphysics, are not *your* province. Machiavel, Newton, Euclid, Malebranche, or Locke, would lie with a very ill grace in *your* closets. They would render you *unwomanly* indeed. They would damp that vivacity, and destroy that disengaged ease and softness, which are the very essence of your graces.

" 'The *elegant* studies are, more immediately, your department. They do not require so much time, abstraction or comprehensiveness of mind— they bring no wrinkles, and they will give a polish to your manners, and such a liberal expansion to your understanding as every rational creature should endeavour to attain.

" 'Whilst men, with solid judgment and a superior *vigour*, are to combine ideas, to discriminate and examine a subject to the bottom, *you* are to give it all its *brilliancy* and all its charms. *They* provide the furniture; you dispose it with propriety. They build the house; you are to fancy and ornament the ceiling.' "

The ceiling is too much even for Aunt Ruth, who joins in the general laughter. "Do go on, Aunt Rachel," I urge, "and tell us what sort of literature he suggests to ornament the ceiling."

"Well," continues Aunt Rachel, "here in letter 45 he enumerates the *Spectator,* the *Tatler,* the *Guardian,* the *Rambler,* the *Adventurer,* and the *World.* Addison, he says, he puts at the head of the list, because that writer 'more frequently than any of the rest, gives lessons of morality and prudence to the sex, and, for delicacy of sentiment, is peculiarly adapted to female reading.' I see that he suggests also in the same letter the advisability of conversation with intelligent people, because conversation 'gives us all the graces of intelligence without its austerities; its depth without its wrinkles. It gently *agitates* the sedentary frame and gives a brisker motion to the blood and spirits.' "

"But what about poetry?" I insist. "Surely he must make poetry the chief ornament of the ceiling."

"Well, I am not so sure of that," answers Aunt Rachel, as she turns the pages. "Ah, here it is.

" 'Poetry,' he says in letter 58, 'I do not wish you to cultivate further than to possess a relish for its beauties. Verses, if not excellent, are execrable indeed. The muses live upon a *mount,* and there is no enjoying any of their favours unless you can climb to the height of Parnassus.

" 'Besides, a passion for poetry is dangerous to a woman. It heightens her natural sensibility to an extravagant degree and frequently inspires such a romantic turn of mind as is utterly inconsistent with the solid duties and proprieties of life.' "

"But if he doesn't wish you to ornament the ceiling with your own effusions," I insist, "doesn't he at least suggest a few frescoes from the accepted poets?"

"Yes," replies Aunt Rachel. "I have it. Letter 59 recommends Shakespeare because his plays 'will give you a useful fund of historical information'; Paradise Lost 'because Milton, above all other authors, describes the distinguishing graces of the sex'; Homer in Pope's translation, and Virgil in Dryden's; and—Upon my word! *Whom* do you think he includes as the only other member of this hierarchy? No other than the forgotten William Mason, whose 'Caractacus, Elfrida, and English Garden, have acquired him considerable celebrity.'

"But, see! The next chapter adds to the list: Miss Seward who 'is a star of the first magnitude'; Miss Hannah More, whose 'Bleeding Rock, Search after Happiness, Sir Eldred of the Bower, Sacred Dramas, Female Fables, etc., will please and instruct you'; Miss Williams' *Peru;* Miss Charlotte Smith whom 'the muses will in time raise to a considerable eminence'; the Comtesse le Genlis; Lord

Lyttleton; Akenside; and Cowper, whose poems he very mildly praises as 'calculated to do considerable service.' But the grand climax of his list is reached in the closing paragraph: 'The most finished poet of the age is Hayley. His Essay on History and on Epic Poetry, his Ode to Howard, and his Triumphs of Temper, have received very great and very general applause.'

"The following chapters, I see," continues Aunt Rachel, "recommend books on travel, on geography, on art, on heraldry, and what not; but here he comes back once more to his ideal woman:

" 'But after all this recommendation of different studies, do not mistake me. I do not want to make you a fine writer, an historian, a naturalist, a geographer, an astronomer, a poet, a painter, a connoisseur, or a virtuoso of any kind. But I would have you to possess such a *general* knowledge as will usefully and innocently fill up your leisure hours, raise your taste above fantastic levities, and render you an agreeable friend and acquaintance.' "

Aunt Rachel is about to lay the Letters aside, but I remind her of the "Accomplishments" and "Prudential Conduct" which the preface promised. She yields and turning here and there among the pages of the Letters, with an assumed gravity, through which I can catch the twinkle of a merry eye, reads these highly italicized paragraphs from the "Character" of a model girl.

" '*Another distinguishing grace* of Louisa, is

softness. She is (what *nature* intended her to be) *wholly* a woman. She has a quality, that is the direct opposite to *manliness and vigour.* Her voice is gentle; her pronunciation delicate; her passions are never suffered to be *boisterous.* She never talks politics; she never foams with anger; she is seldom seen in any *masculine* amusements; she does not practise *archery.* I will venture to prophesy that she will never canvass for votes at an election. I never saw her in an unfeminine dress, or her features discomposed with *play.* She *really* trembles with the apprehension of danger. She feels *unaffectedly* for every person exposed to it. A friend leaving her father's house, only for a short time, calls forth her concern. The farewell tear stands big in its transparent sluice. . . . The heart of this lovely girl is all over *sympathy and softness.* The big tear trembles in her eye, on every trying occasion.

" 'From Louisa's strict confinement and systematic life you would conclude, perhaps, that she had almost contracted a *disrelish* for books. But, indeed, it is far otherwise; her studies are her pleasure; they are so judiciously mixed with entertainment, and so interwoven, as it were, with the common casual occurrences of the day, that she considers them more as an *amusement,* than a *business.* Her private moments, when she is left to her own choice, are not infrequently beguiled with the very same employments which had engrossed the other parts of the day.

" 'The garden is the scene where she indulges all the luxury of her taste; and her rambles into it are as frequent as the great variety of her avocations will permit. One day I found her in this

retirement. The place was very happily fancied.
Large clumps of trees, on both sides, with their
intervening foliage had rendered it impervious to
any human eye. Nature had wantoned with particular luxuriance. A clear transparent spring mur-
mured through the valley. And it was fenced, on
both sides, with a very lofty mound, cast up as on
purpose, and planted with perennial shrubs. A
shady arbour in the middle, catching through a
beautiful vista the spire of the village church, in-
vited to meditation and repose. She was reclined
here rather in a pensive attitude, reading Burke's
Essays on the Beautiful and Sublime: and to me
she appeared, I must confess, more enchanting,
more *beautiful* and more *sublime*, than the admired
work of that well-known and admired author.' "

"Now, that landscape picture," puts in Aunt
Ruth, "used to seem to me the most exquisite thing!
I always thought that if I had the money some day,
I should look until I found just such a scene, and
buy it and recline there just as Louisa did, for
reading and meditation. I do not seem to care for
it so much to-day. I am afraid you are not reading
it very sympathetically, Rachel;—or perhaps I am
growing old."

But Aunt Rachel continues:

" 'On another occasion . . . . she had stolen
from the domestic circle to indulge, at leisure, soli-
tary grief. The book she held in her hand was Lord
Lyttleton's Dialogues of the Dead. The soft
melancholy visible in her countenance, the very
apparent agitation of her spirits, and the grief,

bursting through her animated eyes, formed a very interesting whole. . . .

" 'A third time of her elopement, she was reading the only novel which she permits herself to read, that of Sir Charles Grandison. Tears like an April shower tinged with the sun, were mingled with her joy. The book was opened where the once amiable Harriet Byron is *now* Lady Grandison; where the painful suspense of her virtuous though premature attachment, is crowned by an eternal union with its object, and she is kneeling to her ever-venerable grandmother, to implore a blessing. Heavens! (said she) What an exquisite and inimitable painter was Richardson. . . . I never read this writer without weeping. He had an amazing talent for the pathetic and descriptive. He opens all the sluices of tenderness, and tears flow down our cheeks like a river. . . . If *all* novels had been written on such a plan, they would, doubtless, have been very excellent vehicles of wisdom and goodness.

" 'The *last* time I broke in upon Louisa's retirement, she was surrounded with authors. She seemed bent upon indulging her elegant taste, in all its extravagance.

" 'Addison's papers on the Pleasures of Imagination; several pieces of Miss Seward; Mason's English Garden; Ariosto, with Hoole's translation, and Webb's Inquiry into the Beauties of Painting, together with a Collection of Poems, lay, in promiscuous dignity, beside her. She has accustomed herself to enter into a sort of commonplace-book, passages which she thinks particularly striking. I am happy in being able to give you a little specimen of her choice, for she indulged me with a sight of the valuable manuscript.

" 'The first poetical rose she had plucked was from——' "

"Oh, don't, don't, Aunt Rachel," I cry, "I shall dissolve in tears if you go on with Louisa's dew-besprinkled posy. Look ahead and tell us what the amiable gentleman says about matrimony."

"Matrimony? M—n—M—n. Yes. Lucy must not marry an old man or a country squire or a military man or a lawyer.

" 'Beware of *such* society; beware of your *heart*. Let not the unblushing front of a barrister, let not the mere scarlet habit of a *petit maître* who has studied the windings of the female heart infinitely more than tactics, or the art of war, let not a few civil sayings, or flattering attentions beguile your *imagination*, or lay your *prudence* asleep.' The best thing for Lucy to do, he believes, is to marry a clergyman. 'A man of *this* cast seems particularly calculated not only to *relish*, but to *enhance* the happiness of the married state.' "

"Good for the *Reverend* John Bennett!" I murmur.

"As for the rest of his advice to Lucy," continues Aunt Rachel, "there doesn't seem to be anything worth—but wait. Here's a paragraph that fairly bristles with italics. He is indulging in the hypothetical case of Lucy's loving a man who does not return her affection:

" 'If any man therefore, can *deliberately* be so

cruel as to visit you frequently and show you every particularity that is only short of this *grand* explanation, never see him in private; and, if that be insufficient, and you *still* feel tender sentiments towards him, determine to shun his company *forever*. It is easier, remember, to extinguish a fire that has *just* broken out, than one which has been gathering strength and *violence* from a long concealment. Many have neglected this necessary precaution, and died silent *martyrs* to their fondness and imprudence. The eye of beauty has *languished* in solitude, or been dimmed with a flood of *irremediable* tears. The heart has throbbed with *unconquerable* tumults, which *gradually* have dissolved an *elegant* frame, that deserved a much *better* fate. Undiscovered by the physician, they have baffled all the resources of his skill; they have rendered ineffectual all the tenderness of friends, and *death* alone has administered that ease, which neither beauty, friends, nor fortune could bestow.' ''

"Now, Rachel, I protest," interrupts Aunt Ruth. "You are laughing!" And even in the subdued glow of the candles which light the Dark Room I fancy I can catch a glimpse of a tear "standing big in the transparent sluice" of Aunt Ruth's eye.

At any rate, Aunt Rachel suddenly closes the book, and, ignoring my plea for some choice extracts from *The Young Maiden,* begins to take down other books from the shelves, putting them, now in the "junk" pile which is accumulating on the floor, now on a table to be preserved against the time when some new-fangled sectional book-case shall receive them.

I catch a glimpse of Fénelon's *Télémaque,* much worn, on its way to the junk pile and rescue it to read myself.

"We read it in our 'Seminary' days," explains Aunt Ruth. "A little Latin and much French were we taught. Harriet Hawkins, who has a daughter in college, tells me that Jeanette is expected to be proficient in Greek and German. It was not so with us."

Bertha the Beauty, by Letitia E. L. Jenkins, Author of Heart Drops from Memory's Urn is smilingly consigned to the junk-heap by Aunt Rachel; and my look of enquiry wins no comment. From the same quarter I rescue *The Parlor Scrapbook for 1836* and find that one of the "Choice Selections" included between its covers is "The Favourite of the Harem, with Oriental Illustrations." That too is allowed to pass. At *Duychinck's National Portrait Gallery,* in a series of paper bound folio volumes, I cast a wishful eye. One volume opens to steel engravings of Hannah More, Maria Edgeworth, and Napoleon Bonaparte resting comfortably side by side, and I am tempted to go on;— but Duychinck is laid on the table. A little leather bound copy of *Virgil's Bucolics and Georgics* with interlinear translation, 1833, shares the fate of *Bertha the Beauty*; and I pause to reflect that the youthful scholar of three generations ago, like his great-grandson, had his "pony". Did they call it an "ambling pad nag" in those days, I wonder.

For a while, I am put to tearing the title pages out of discarded school books of nobody knows how long ago, lest the curious eye of the junk-man should read the inscriptions thereon. The books are uninteresting things, but, Oh! the names! the names! Scrawled there in faded ink or almost obliterated pencil! Men who were boys once, like me, and who passed from the immature scrawl of boyhood to the prime vigour of manhood, and who grew old and died—and whose very burial places have been levelled to the surrounding sod, and been forgotten. And here is the name of one of whom my grandmother used to tell me when I was a little boy. A merry little chap, he was, this great-uncle of mine. Fate took him from his grammar and spelling books; and to me who have never seen him, he will always remain what my childhood pictured him—a happy little Dream of a lad who never had to grow up.

But the old book closet is almost emptied now; and among the last of the books lying there, Aunt Ruth picks up a frayed leather folio. "Volume three of *The Christian Baptist*," she says. "That magazine was published by Alexander Campbell. He founded the sect of Campbellites, you remember, Ned; and we used to read *The Christian Baptist* with much interest in those days." "Yes," I assent, and as I dutifully pick up the volume, it opens to a lock of short black hair neatly pressed between its pages. The colour heightens in Aunt

Ruth's face; and Aunt Rachel's smile is a bit slow in coming. My eyes speak the question which my lips hesitate to frame.

But Aunt Ruth takes up one candle and Aunt Rachel the other, and we shut the book-closet doors upon empty shelves, and go downstairs together.

THE PREFACE

A preface is more than an author can resist, for it is the reward of his labours. When the foundation stone is laid, the architect appears with his plans, and struts for an hour before the public eye. So with the writer in his preface: he may have never a word to say, but he must show himself for a moment in the portico, hat in hand, and with an urbane demeanour.—ROBERT LOUIS STEVENSON, *An Inland Voyage.*

GOOD old Jeremy Taylor, in the preface to *A Dissuasive from Popery,* tells the story of a "Roman Gentleman [who] had to please himself written a book in Greek and presented it to Cato; he desired him to pardon the faults of his expressions, since he wrote in Greek, which was a tongue in which he was not perfect Master. Cato told him he had better then to have let it alone, and written in Latine, by how much it is better not to commit a fault than to make apologies. For if the thing be good, it needs not to be excus'd, if it be not good, a crude apologie will do nothing but confess the fault, but never make amends." Whereupon the Lord Bishop of Down, pointing the moral of his own tale, devotes eleven pages to his prefatory apologies.

The case is typical; for forewords, be they the

poetic prologue of the drama, or the prose pre-
liminaries of philosopher, poet, essayist, or novelist,
are not infrequently fraught with more danger to
the author than is the book which they would excuse. *Hours of Idleness,* had it appeared anony-
mously, might have won at least the safety of
oblivion, and the noble author might have been
spared more than one *mauvais quart d'heure.* But
young George Gordon, Lord Byron, wrote a preface
apologizing for his poetry on the score of his youth
and inexperience, and quite went out of his way to
provide a peg for the Edinburgh reviewer to hang
a gibe on.

"As an extenuation of this offence" [the publication of the poem] remarks Brougham in the
Edinburgh, "the noble author is peculiarly forward
in pleading minority. . . . Much stress is laid upon
it in the preface, and the poems are connected with
this general statement of the case by particular
dates substantiating the age at which each was
written. Now the law upon the point of minority,
we hold to be perfectly clear. It is a plea available
only to the defendant; no plaintiff can offer it as a
supplementary ground of action. Thus, if any suit
could be brought against Lord Byron for the purpose of compelling him to put into court a certain
quantity of poetry; and if judgment were given
against him; it is highly probable that an exception
would be taken, were he to deliver *for poetry* the
contents of this volume. To this, he might plead
minority; but as he now makes voluntary tender
of the article, he hath no right to sue, on that

ground, for the price in good current praise, should the goods be unmarketable. This is our view of the law on the point, and, we dare to say, so will it be ruled. Perhaps however, in reality, all that he tells us about his youth is rather with a view to increase our wonder than to soften our censures. He possibly means to say, 'See how a minor can write! This poem was actually composed by a young man of eighteen, and this by one of only sixteen!'"

O acrid Brougham! O writhing Noble Minor! One can imagine the young poet wishing that he had been compelled, like exiled Ovid, to say: *Sine me, liber, ibis in urbem.*

No less fatal was Keats' deprecatory plea when *Endymion* was offered to the world.

"Knowing within myself," he says, "the manner in which this poem has been produced, it is not without a feeling of regret that I make it public.— What manner I mean will be quite clear to the reader, who must perceive great inexperience, immaturity, and every error denoting a feverish attempt, rather than a deed accomplished."

On this boyish apology the fiend of the *Quarterly* seizes with avidity; but it is a subsequent admission which seals the author's doom. "The two first books, and indeed the two last, I feel sensible are not of such completion as to warrant their passing the press." Here indeed is an opening in the victim's wavering guard. "*Je touche,*" cries Mr. Reviewer-Cyrano, triumphantly. "Thus 'the two first books' are, even in his [Keats'] own judgment, unfit to appear, and 'the two last' are, it seems, in the same condition,—and as two and two make four, and as that is the whole number of books, we have a clear and, we believe, a very just estimate of the entire work."

Nor is it unusual for the author quite unconsciously to suggest in his prefatory remarks the basis for the most deservedly severe criticism of his work. The creator of Peter Bell and the Idiot Boy never came to realize that he was programme-ridden, and that much of his best writing was done when he was most oblivious of his thesis. The preface to the *Lyrical Ballads* was not only an epoch-making *pronunciamento*; it was also a confession of a mechanical method. To Wordsworth's way of thinking the poems of the edition of 1798 were not primarily poems; they were *experiments,* —written "chiefly with a view to ascertain how far" (in his now famous phrase) "the language of conversation in the middle and lower classes of society is adapted to the purposes of poetic pleasure."

Just two years before the future English Laureate pronounced his arduous programme, a Scottish poet brought to its troubled close a life whose ideal had been much the same,—who had done because he could not help it what Wordsworth did because it could be done. Oddly the prefatory explanations contrast.

"None of the following works," Burns had written in the preface to the collection of 1786, "were ever composed with a view to the press. To amuse myself with the little creations of my own fancy, amid the toils and fatigues of a laborious life; to transcribe the various feelings, the loves, the griefs, the hopes, the fears in my own breast; to find some kind of counterpoise to the struggles of a world, always an alien scene, a task uncouth to the poetical mind,—these were my motives for courting the muses, and in these I found poetry its own reward."

But if the preface has occasionally served no higher purpose than to furnish a theme for the "chorus of insolent reviewers" or to point out the weak spots in the champion's armour, it has also at times thrown more than one fascinating sidelight upon the personality of the author. It has not infrequently been a medium of naïve self-confession, as when Charles Kingsley, setting out to write an historical novel of fifth-century Christianity, confesses to his somewhat prudish public that though he has endeavoured "to sketch the age, its manners, and its literature" as he found them, his Anglican conscience has rather balked at telling the whole truth. "Oh, don't be shocked at this or that,"—so Mr. Gosse rather flippantly interprets the author's preface. "It is nothing to what I could tell you if I chose. You think that Orestes was a very wicked man, do you? Shall I make your flesh creep by explaining,—but no, I won't; your dear little Early Victorian ears wouldn't stand it."

Or, to make a leap back over the centuries, one

finds Lord Berners, in the prologue to his translation of *The Hystorye of the moost noble and valiaunt Knyght Arthur of lytell Brytayne*, quaintly admitting that he set out to translate the book before he had read it, and that, as he proceeded, he had been so staggered by its "unpossibilities" that he had more than once been of a mind to lay it down. Treacherous as are the seas upon which he finds himself embarked, however, he takes comfort in the thought that the book has been put together probably "not without some measure of truth and virtuous intent."

One is reminded of Caxton's sceptical preface to the *Morte Darthur*: "For to pass the time, this book shall be pleasant to read in, but for to give faith and belief that all is true that is contained herein, ye be at your liberty." And indeed this same honest Caxton, "simple person" as he confesses himself to be, set type to no better purpose in the *Morte Darthur* itself than in the modest preface with which he gave it to the world:

"Wherefore . . . I have under the simple conning that God hath sent to me, under the favour and correction of all noble lords and gentlemen, enprised to imprint a book of the noble histories of the said King Arthur, and of certain of his knights . . . to the intent that noble men may see and learn the noble acts of chivalry, the gentle and virtuous deeds that some knights used in those days, by which they came to honour, and how they that were vicious were punished and oft put to shame and

rebuke; humbly beseeching all noble lords and
ladies, with all other estates of what other estate or
degree they been of, that shall see and read in this
said book and work, that they take the good and
honest acts in their remembrance, and to follow
the same. Wherein they shall find many joyous
and pleasant histories, and noble and renowned
acts of humanity, gentleness and chivalry. For
herein may be seen noble chivalry, courtesy, humanity, friendliness, hardiness, love, friendship,
cowardice, murder, hate, virtue and sin. Do after
the good and leave the evil, and it shall bring you
to good fame and renommee."

It was with equal sincerity if perhaps less charm
of style that Defoe in his prefaces used to point the
moral of his adventurous yarns. That remarkable
personage, Colonel Jacque,—"who was born a
Gentleman, put 'prentice to a Pick-pocket, flourished six and twenty years as a Thief, and was then
kidnapped to Virginia; came back a Merchant, . . .
went into the Wars, behaved bravely, got preferment, was made Colonel of a Regiment, came over
and fled with the Chevalier, is still Abroad completing a Life of Wonders, and resolves to die a General,"—enjoy his rascality as we may to-day, was
conceived by the author in a spirit of the most
commendable piety.

"The various turns of his fortune in the world
make a delightful field for the reader to wander in;
a garden where he may gather wholesome and
medicinal fruits, none noxious or poisonous; where

he will see virtue and the ways of wisdom everywhere applauded, honoured, encouraged, rewarded; vice and all kinds of wickedness attended with misery, many kinds of infelicities; and at last, sin and shame going together, the persons meeting with reproof and reproach, and the crimes with abhorrence.

"Every wicked reader" [this is refreshing; the class has apparently ceased to exist to-day] "will here be encouraged to a change, and it will appear that the best and only good end of an impious, misspent life is repentance; that in this there is comfort, peace and oftentimes hope, and that the penitent shall be returned like the prodigal, *and his latter end be better than his beginning.*"

The italics are Defoe's,—which leaves no doubt about his pious intentions, whatever we may think of the fact that, so far as the book is concerned, the beginning is much better than the latter end. The old Adam in Defoe rather loses zest in the redoubtable Colonel after the latter's reformation is effected.

But not all the prefaces of former times are marked by such a sweet humility as Caxton's or such a worthy piety as Defoe's. Burly Ben Jonson is never burlier than in the poetic forewords to his plays; and in the first of them—that the prologue of *Every Man in his Humour* may have been composed at a later date is of no moment—his prefatory remarks are of no uncertain tenor. Not for him the base truckling of those poets who would serve the "ill customs of the age." Rather

> ". . . be pleased to see
> One such to-day as other plays should be,—"

wherein, instead of the crudities and impossibilities of the romantic drama, you shall find

> "Deeds and language such as men do use,
> And persons such as comedy would choose."

Izaak Walton, as became his calling, was not so self-assertive as the author of *Every Man in his Humour,* but he is every whit as indifferent to criticism; and nowhere in the *Compleat Angler* proper is the cool self-sufficiency of the true brother of the angle better brought out than in these words from the preface:

> "And though this Discourse may be liable to some exceptions, yet I cannot doubt but that most Readers may receive so much pleasure or profit by it, as may make it worthy the time of their perusal, if they be not too grave or too busy men. . . . And I wish the Reader also to take notice, that in writing of it, I have made myself a recreation of a recreation; and that it may prove so to him, and not read dull and tediously, I have in several places mixed, not any scurrility, but some innocent, harmless mirth, of which, if thou be a severe, sour complexioned man, then I here disallow thee to be a competent judge."

"A recreation of a recreation!"—happy the man who can confess to such a cheerful spontaneity of composition! So Bunyan, in the quaintly rhymed preface to *Pilgrim's Progress*, testifies that the work was done, "mine own self to gratifie:"—

> "But yet I did not think
> To show to all the World my Pen and Ink
> In such a mode; I only thought to make
> I knew not what: nor did I undertake
> Thereby to please my neighbour; no, not I.
> I did it mine own self to gratifie.
>   . . . And so I penned
> It down, until at last it came to be
> For length and breadth the bigness which you see.
> Well, when I had thus put mine ends together,
> I shew'd them others, that I might see whether
> They would condemn them or them justifie:
> And some said, Let them live; some, Let them die.
> Some said, *John*, print it; others said, Not so;
> Some said, It might do good; others said, No.
> Now was I in a straight, and did not see
> Which was the best thing to be done by me:
> At last, I thought, Since you are thus divided,
> I print it will; and so the case decided."

When Ben Jonson blustered, he also "made good"; and Bunyan could afford to thank Providance that his neighbour's "John, print it," had decided his uncertain course; but it is not uncommon to follow the preface through its throes of parturition only to find that the product is little more than a ridiculous mouse.   Dr. Johnson's cynical reference to his early instructor in English, who "published a spelling book and dedicated it to the universe," will be remembered; and I have before

me an ancient grammar which makes its bow to
the waiting world with no less pomposity. Published in Cambridge, Massachusetts, in 1854, it
purports to be "A Compendious Treatise on the
Languages English, Latin, Greek, German, Spanish,
and French, founded on the immutable principle
of the relation which one word sustains to another."
By way of frontispiece rises a gigantic tree-trunk
from which juts out a massive limb. Upon the
trunk in great black letters is the word "God," and
along the limb in print of equal magnitude are the
words "hath spoken." "God hath spoken!" Could
a more effective preface be imagined? It is true
that, upon closer examination, lettered twigs de-
volving from trunk and limb resolve themselves
into a pictorial grammatical analysis of the first
verse of the first chapter of Hebrews; but the prim-
ary impression, the awful sensation of *Jupiter
tonans*, remains unimpaired.

The worthy author of this forgotten grammar
threw the responsibility for its fate upon the Al-
mighty, with apparently no doubt that, between
author and Sponsor, the days of the *Compendious
Treatise* would be long in the land. Other and more
mundane support had he, too, for upon the fly-
leaves clusters a very muster-roll of the great names
of his day,—Millard Fillmore, H. Clay, Winfield
Scott, William H. Seward, Hamilton Fish, Bayard
Taylor, Henry W. Longfellow, Jared Sparks, and a
score of others—all the signatures in unmistakably

authentic facsimile. With such stately inaugural the *Compendious Treatise* takes its oath of office. How the little barefooted poets and novelists-to-be must have climbed the lamp posts to catch a glimpse of the majestic figure! How the man who had been made Laureate of England four years before, had chance of traffic brought a copy to his hand,—how Tennyson would have smiled! and perhaps turned back musingly to the preface of a thin little volume entitled *Poems by Two Brothers,*—"Haec novimus esse nihil" had been its modest motto,—and the preface: "We have passed the Rubicon and we leave the rest to fate, though its edict may create a fruitless regret that we ever emerged from the shade and courted notoriety."

The prefatory pronouncement of the *Compendious Treatise* had at least the merit of brevity; and, indeed, unless the nature of the case calls for an elaborate disquisition, or unless, as in the case of Scott, the book in question has already won a recognition which warrants unlimited personalia, the proud author has generally been content to "show himself for a moment in the portico," and then turn the public loose in his vaulted corridors. "If brevity is the soul of wit anywhere, it is most especially so in a preface," remarks Dickens, who did live up to this principle in his prefaces, however he violated it in his stories: "firstly, because those who do not read such things as prefaces prefer them, like grace before meat, in an epigrammatic form; and secondly, because nine hundred and ninety-nine people out of every thousand never read a preface at all;" and to this brevity the hopeful author must add a special savour of personality, if he do not wish to be a candidate for the obliviousness of the nine hundred and ninety-nine. It is the rare preface which inspires in the breast of the reader the hope of Nick Bottom, the weaver,—"I shall desire you of more acquaintance, good Master Cobweb."

After all, it was a fellow countryman and contemporary of the forgotten author of the *Compendious Treatise* who could most skilfully compound his prefaces of these two indispensable elements, and put the gentle reader into the best possible humour with himself, the world, the author, and the volume in hand; and of Dr. Holmes's many genial prefaces, one likes best to recall that which ushered the delightful series of Autocrat papers to an audience even larger than the *Atlantic* could furnish. "I cannot make the book over again," wrote the old Doctor, twenty-five years after the papers had appeared in the magazine, "and I will not try to mend old garments with new cloth. Let the sensible reader take it for granted that the author would agree with him in changing whatever he would alter; in leaving out whatever he would omit."

Could anything be more urbane?

A DIPLOMATIC APPRAISAL

"MEMORIALS of King Henry the Seventh" issued under the authority of the Master of the Rolls as a part of *The Chronicles and Memorials of Great Britain and Ireland during the Middle Ages*. How solid and substantial it looks, the portly volume, there among the dun rows of State Papers on the library shelves! Dusty-brown field for the source-hunter to plod in; no "human interest" here, surely. And yet—

What a pother the novelist is always in, to visualize his heroine,—to describe a pretty girl so that you can really see her! "The blush that gloried Luna when she kissed the shepherd on the hills of Latmos," exclaims Thomas Lodge, "was not tainted with such a pleasant dye, as the vermilion flourished on the silver hue of Rosalind's countenance; her eyes were like those lamps that make the wealthy covert of the heavens more gorgeous, sparkling favour and disdain." And then the poor novelist gives it up, and dodges. "What should I need to decipher her particular beauties, when by the censure of all she was the paragon of all earthly perfection?"

And if a sixteenth century novelist who was beginning to get a little practice in the art of descrip-

tion couldn't do any better than this, imagine the
predicament of three elderly gentlemen of the court
of Henry Seventh who suddenly found themselves
entrusted by their royal master with the duty of
describing a pretty girl so that he, the King, could
see her with his mind's eye. No chance for euphu-
istic extravagances here.

Yes, it is all in the dry-as-dust Memorials of
Henry Seventh. Henry's Queen, Elizabeth of York,
had died two years before; and Henry bethought
himself of seeking a matrimonial alliance with the
young Queen of Naples, widow of Ferdinand the
Second. Diplomatically, the alliance appeared to
be an excellent one; but certain information had to
be privily obtained, before the royal courtship could
be formally announced; and Henry forthwith sent
three ambassadors to the court of Naples, who carried with them a body of categorical instructions
curiously typical of a king who was half a miser
and half a poet. The ambassadors were to disguise
their actual mission—through what pretence is
apparently left to their own invention; and they
were to ascertain whether the young Queen was
blessed, first, with wealth, and, second, with come-
liness. As to the first, they needed no detailed instructions. There is nothing ambiguous about
pounds, shillings and pence. But the second was a
different matter. A kodak, unobtrusively used,
might have solved the problem; but for that, Henry
was born a thought too soon. A painted portrait

would have helped. They were authorized to get
one, if it could be had; but they could not openly
ask the young queen to sit, and they reported that
they could in no wise find or secure any portrait
already executed.

It was doubtless with the thought of failure in
this direction that the king forestalled, or, at least,
poor man, tried to forestall, the limitations of a
diplomatic vocabulary, by providing them with a
series of questions—perhaps specifications would be
a better word—in regard to the young queen's come-
liness. Being a discriminating monarch himself,
and having probably had his three ambassadors
under observation at court on more than one occasion, he tried to leave nothing to chance or to any
accidental ebullitions of descriptive power on the
part of his official observers. In this, he did wisely.
I am convinced that the ambassadors were elderly
gentlemen, whose imaginations, if they had ever
had any, had been permitted to fade into the light
of common day. They probably had never read
Chaucer; and Malory too, with his occasional evo-
cations of feminine beauty, was in all likelihood a
sealed book to them. Even with the help of Henry's
searching questions, they were destined to fare
badly enough. The century in which they had come
to manhood had been rather a lean one in literary
art, and they were no better than their neighbours.
A few years before they started on their difficult
mission, Caxton was lamenting the inadequacy of

the English language; and when they got to Naples and perused their instructions, they were in a position to sympathize with him. There is something irresistibly comic in the spectacle of these three solemn gentlemen, with their legal phrases, their carefully qualifying clauses, their quidlibets and quodlibets, trying to tell the king, not merely how pretty she was, but also how she was pretty—which, may it please you, is quite a different matter.

It was in the audience chamber at the court of Valencia that they saw her first. In the centre of the room there was "a great carpet spread, whereon by the window-side sat the old queen, and on her left hand from the window-wardes sat the young queen. Both the said queens were clothed in black cloth and also in black kerchowes as mourners, and in like case were all they that waited on the said queens." Among these were Duke Fernandin of Naples, several Duchesses and Countesses, "and other ladies and gentlemen to the number of XVIIj or XXtie persons."

The difficulties which the ambassadors had on this occasion are typical of those which they encountered in the other formal audiences which they describe. In response to Henry's "Item" as to whether the young queen's "countenance be cheerful and amiable, frowning or melancholy, stedfast or light, or blushing in communication," all that they can say is that she "is not light nor boldhardy in speech, but with a demure, womanly, shamefaced countenance, and of few words as that we could perceive, as we can think that she uttered the fewer words because that the queen her mother was present, which had all the sayings." What could the three gentlemen make of that Item, if the loquacious old queen insisted on having "all the sayings"?

As to the young queen's face, they are instructed to report "whether it be painted or not, and whether it be fat or lean, sharp or round." The first item is fortunately reported in the negative. Of the general aspect of her countenance, the best that they can do is that "the favour of her visage is after her stature, of a very good compass, and amiable and somewhat round and fat."

Up to this point, our reporters have fared pretty well; but when it comes to a more precise particularizing of her "points"—for the questions are mercilessly minute—they are compelled to qualify their statements with caution worthy of a lawyer. The queen "is very fair and clear of skin, as far as that we could perceive by her visage, neck and hands, the which we saw and well perceived." As to the colour, or as the Item has it, the "colours" of her hair, the caution is even greater. "As to this article, by that we could see and perceive by the brows of the said queen, and by the ends of some of her hairs that we perceived through her kerchowes, it should seem her hair to be a brown hair of colour." In response to the "Item, to note well her eyes, brows, teeth and lips," they risk an unqualified opinion, and even venture a simile—a simile, by the way, which was later to become a favourite one among the euphuists: "As to this article, the eyes of the said queen be of colour brown, somewhat greyish; and her brows of a brown hair and very small, like a wire of hair; and her teeth fair and clean, and as far as we could perceive, well set." After all, it is to be observed that they do not forget their caution. "We will commit ourselves," they seem to say, "as to her front teeth. But as to her molars, since they were not visible to us, Your Majesty cannot expect us to venture an opinion."

In regard to "the fashion of her nose," there is a momentary return to confidence. "As to this article, the fashion of her nose is a little rising in the midward, and a little coming or bowing towards the end, and she is much like-nosed unto the queen her mother." This is not bad, though one is inclined to doubt how much the king was illuminated by the likeness to the maternal nose, which was equally unknown to him. When it comes to "the height and breadth of her forehead," the honest gentlemen are positively craven. "And as to the forehead, the height or the breadth thereof we could not perfectly discern, for the manner of the wearing of the kerchowes or tuckas in that country is such that a man cannot well judge it, for their kerchowes coming down to their brows, and much the less we could come by the very knowledge of that cause for that the queen weared black kerchowes."

They may not be blessed with a sense of humour, these worthy gentlemen, but they have a laborious persistence which probably served them better in other causes. They can report on "whether the palm of her hand be thick or thin, and whether her hands be fat or lean, long or short," because they have seen "the hands of the said queen bare at three sundry times, that we kissed her said hands," and their report on this item is entirely satisfactory. Thanks to the same occasions, they are able to give a satisfactory report on "whether her fingers be long or short, small or great, broad or narrow before." In response to a highly particularized query as to her neck, however, they can only report with diplomatic discretion that "it is not very short and not very long, but seemeth for to be shorter because that her breasts be fully and somewhat big." The fact that her breasts are "trussed somewhat high causeth her grace for to seem much the fullyer."

Concerning another important item, their failure is complete, and they confess it like the honest gentlemen they are: "Item, That they endeavour them to speak with the young queen fasting, and that she may tell unto them some matter at length, and to approach as near to her mouth as they honestly may, to the intent that they may feel the condition of her breath, whether it be sweet or not, and to mark at every time when they speak with her if they feel any savour of spices, rosewater or musk by the breath of her mouth or not."

To this article (halitosis being yet unborn) :

"We could never come unto the speech of the said queen fasting, wherefore we could nor might not attain to knowledge of that part of this article, notwithstanding at such other times as we have spoken and had communication with the said queen, we have approached as nigh unto her visage as that conveniently we might do, and we could feel no savour of any spices or waters, and we think verily by the favour of her visage and cleanness of her complexion and of her mouth that the said queen is like for to be of a sweet savour and well eyred."

They are instructed to report on "the manner of her diet, whether she be a great feeder or drinker;" and after inquiry from the household servants and "one Pastorell, her apothecary," they make a favourable statement; and finally, they deal with an item which, curiously enough, proved to be the most perplexing of all. Both question and answer deserve quotation in full.

"Item, to note the height of her stature, and to inquire whether she wear any slippers, and of what height her slippers be, to the intent they be not deceived in the very height and stature of her; and if they may come to the sight of her slippers, then to note the fashion of her foot.

"As to this article, of the height and stature of

the said young queen, it is answered that we could not come by the perfect knowledge of her height, forasmuch as that her grace weareth slippers after the manner of her country, whereof we saw the fashion, the which be of vj fingers breadth, of height large, and her foot after the proportion of the same is but small, but by the slipper the greatness of her foot cannot be known, notwithstanding by the height of her slipper, considering the height that she appeared unto our sight being a-foot, her grace seemed not to be of high stature and also by cause of the manner of the clothing that women do use and wear after the manner of the country, and also she of herself is somewhat round and well liking, the which causeth her grace for to seem lesser in height."

What a breathless, incoherent pother the poor men were in! If only some Shakespeare of the moment could have been with them to report: "She is just as high as your majesty's heart!"

History does not record what Henry said to the ambassadors when they got home. If Henry had read Chaucer's description of the Prioresse, he probably intimated in diplomatic language that the poet had told more in a dozen lines than those worthy gentlemen, with all their blanks to fill in, had been able to tell in as many pages. But perhaps Henry did not even read the report, before it was deposited in the archives: for the truth is that there was one other item, with which the ambassadors were quite competent to deal, which rendered all their painstaking labours of no avail.

Dr. James Gairdner (editor of the *Memorials*) dryly gives the story its quietus. The young queen, brown-haired, amiable, fragrant and comely, had no money. The deal was off.

* * * *

Since this essay was printed (1916), the document which it describes has been included in G. G. Coulton's volume of excerpts, *Life in the Middle Ages*, vol. iii, Cambridge Press (1929).

THE ARMOURY: A FANTASY

" AND you can still hear them, you tell me—
the bursting bombs, the screams of the great
shells? Your nerves have not recovered yet, and in
your dreams you are still on that

> " . . . . darkling plain,
> Swept with confus'd alarms of struggle and
> flight."

And yet you long to be back, and find your period
of convalescence irksome? You can think of nothing, talk of nothing, but war and the making of
war, and all the while your tired nerves cry out for
rest and quiet? Content you, Sir. Will you come
with me, for a little, to a quiet place I know of,—
quiet and peaceful now, and yet full of the relics
of those heroisms that you love? Here is a door
ajar. Come with me into the Armoury.

"Ah, Sir, be not surprised at these rich carven
panels, and at the rafters of ancient oak. Rather
forget what is outside of that door; forget even that
the door itself, which is unmistakably hewn oak
within, looked like painted pine without. Let your
forgetting be comprehensive, and make yourself at
home. That song of Will Shakespeare's—

'Tell me where is Fancy bred,
  Or in the heart or in the head?—'

which we can hear faintly tinkled on a spinet to a
right Elizabethan air—that song shall magic us
wholly away from the outside world. The good
Poet was speaking of Love, no doubt; but we shall
interpret his fancy as we choose, while you look
with me along the walls of this mine Armoury.

"Here now is the wall of Swords. A goodly
array, is't not? I see you gaze with interest upon
that long blade that heads the line. No wonder
that you admire it, for the pommel and haft are all
of precious stones. Time was, as a good book tells
us, it gave light like thirty torches, but its bright-
ness is somewhat dimmed in these froward times.
You recognize it now, but are puzzled, mayhap, to
find it on these walls. True, Sir, it has not been
wielded in battle since that sad day when Sir
Bedivere took it up and bound the girdle about the
hilts, and threw it as far into the water as he might.
But it was not wholly lost; for I found it in a certain glorious summer of my boyhood, and ever
since it has hung there upon the wall, where the
broken light from yonder narrow window touches
it as with the ray of an autumn sunset. I shall not
soon be parted from it.

"And the sword beside it? 'Tis the one that the
young Galahad lightly plucked from the fleeting
stone, and placed in the waiting scabbard by his

side. Look you at the pommel adorned with jewels, and read the writing wrought thereon with subtle letters of gold: 'Never shall man take me hence but only he by whose side I ought to hang, and he shall be the best knight in the world.' Fair and untarnished is the blade, for all that the young knight slew with it the Seven Deadly Sins. View it ye may, but you nor I nor any of our modern fellowship may touch that spotless steel.

"And the sword beyond it, with the blunted edge? 'Tis Durendal, which Count Roland, in his death-agony, sought vainly to break upon the stone. Charlemagne girded the sword upon him, and with it Roland conquered many a fair province, and slew many a foul Paynim. When Roland entered the Pass of Roncesvalles, he wished a wish which binds us even as we look upon it now. These words he spoke: 'For his liege lord a man ought to suffer all hardship, and endure great heat and cold, and give both his blood and his body. I will smite with Durendal, my good sword that the King gave me. If I die here, may he to whom it shall fall say, "This was the sword of a goodly vassal."' And it is only by the meed of this tribute that Durendal is kept there upon the panel.

"And next it, you observe, hangs Halteclere, which Oliver bore—the good and trusty sword that had not its fellow under heaven save only Durendal. It is good to see them hanging side by side, as if the loyalty of their masters still vibrated

through the steel. Are they thinking, I wonder, of
that heart-stirring cry which Roland uttered to
Oliver at Roncesvalles: 'I will smite with Durendal
my sword, and do thou, Comrade, lay on with Halteclere. Through many lands have we carried
them, and with them have we conquered many a
battle. No ill song must be sung of them.'

"They are the treasure trove of later years, Good
Sir, and there beneath them are two crossed
weapons without which the little group would be
incomplete. One is Joyeuse, the sword of the great
Charles himself. Richly jewelled it is, and encased
in the golden hilt is the tip of the spear with which
Our Lord was pierced upon the Cross. And the
sword of brown steel which lies across it is Almace,
with which the good Bishop Turpin slew some four
hundred Paynims at Roncesvalles.

"But I see that your eye is fixed upon that broad
blade with the strange runes graven in it. 'Tis
Balmung, which Wieland forged and gave to Siegfried. And with it you see the other two swords of
Siegfried's: Gram, the sword of Grief, and Mimung,
the blade which Wittich lent to him. And there
too is Flamborge, the sword of Maugis, which I have
hung so that its point leans over to kiss the blade
of Balmung. The great Wieland forged them both,
and their well-wrought runes croon together of their
ruddy past.

"There are other swords adown the wall which
are good to look upon—Chrysaor, the sword of

Artegall, and Graysteel, and Graban the Grave-digger, and Blutgang the Blood-letter, and Quern-biter, the footbroad sword of King Haakon, and Brinnig the Flaming, which Hildebrand bore—their very names are heartening. But I should detain you too long, were we to stop before each one.

"Rather turn we to the opposite wall, where you perceive the sweet confusion of armour and spears. That great shield which seems to crowd the very rafters—look well upon its intricate tracery: the earth and the sky and the sea, and the sun and the moon and all the stars; and two cities withal, one irradiated with the light of peace and one beclouded with the shadow of war; and the vineyard, with its merry youths and maidens and the boy playing on a harp of gold and singing a pleasant song; and round about the shield the river of Ocean. Yes, in truth, 'tis none other than the shield of Achilles, which Hephæstus wrought him. And there beside it are the corselet brighter than fire and the helmet ridged with gold. And sloping athwart the armour —for you will observe that it is too long to stand erect—is the mighty spear that Cheiron cut on the top of Pelion to be the death of many. Yes, Sir, you are quite right; 'twere as much beyond our puny power to lift that royal weapon, as to draw the stout bow which arches the space beyond. Odysseus brooked no rival in that feat, you remember.

"And no less worthy of your view are those two sturdy shafts which tower side by side on yonder panel. The nearer one with its ebon staff, which Bladud made by magic art of yore, was wielded by the fair Britomart. The farther, of celestial temper, the mighty Ithuriel bore. Why are they placed side by side? Ah, Sir, 'tis a dreamer's whim. Mayhap the causes in which they were wielded were not unlike. Nor is it wholly by chance that yon white shield with a red cross in the midst hangs near the two spears. The shield was Galahad's.

"And now, Sir, I will not detain you longer from the unreal world of everyday affairs which lies beyond the door. Perchance some other day, if you will deign to visit me, we may go together to an ante-room where we shall look upon Antony's sword, Philippan, and Cæsar's yellow blade, Crocea Mors, and the much-dinted iron helmet of Cromwell, and the pathetically tiny suit of armour which a zealous smith wrought for a Stuart kinglet. And perchance too we may peer for a moment into a recess behind a panel, where Don Quixote's basin helmet, and Falstaff's pudding shield, and the arms of Hudibras, lie gathering oblivious dust.

"Ah, Sir, I am sorry to see you go, for it is a rare privilege to renew mine ancient rapture with a congenial spirit. Moreover, there is a chill in the air outside. But here, Sir, allow me to offer you this old cloak which lies upon the window-seat. Do not despise it for its antiquated look, for it hath an excellent history. Jack the Giant-killer received it from his uncle in Cornwall. It is the cloak of Invisibility."

MEDICINE AND ENGLISH LITERATURE

WHY, one wonders, does literature—creative literature, at least—look so often with a jaundiced eye upon the physician? Poetry, fiction, the essay—there is no species of the Belles Lettres which has not been enriched by contributions from that fraternity. Was it not a physician who recently sat upon the official pinnacle of Olympus as Poet Laureate of England? And yet, from Chaucer's *Doctour of Physik* to Bernard Shaw's *The Doctor's Dilemma,* poets, essayists and dramatists alike have taken a shy at the physician.

Long before Molière set the fashion, comedy was wont to burlesque his follies and satirize his foibles. In the mediæval St. George folk-plays, the doctor is a ridiculous figure, riding in, sometimes on a hobby-horse, sometimes on the back of one of his patients, and while he boasts of his skill, bringing St. George back to life by exhibiting a bolus. Elizabethan drama constantly fell foul of him. The Doctor of Physike, who is called in to prescribe for the madness of Lady Macbeth, has at least the merit of sincerity.

"This disease is beyond my practice. . . . .
More needs she the divine than the physician,"

but ordinarily Shakespeare's physicians are Dr. Caiuses, good only for "the abusing of God's patience and the King's English." Ben Jonson never lets slip the opportunity to satirize the profession. Volpone's indictment of the physician anticipates in all essential particulars the bill of complaints which Shaw draws up as a preface to the *Doctor's Dilemma*. "He has no faith in physic," says Mosca of his master, Volpone:

> "He does think
> Most of your doctors are the greatest danger
> And worse disease to escape. . . .
> No sir, nor their fees
> He cannot brook: he says they flay a man
> Before they kill him. . . . .
> And then they do it by experiment
> For which the law not only doth absolve
> But gives them great reward: and he is loth
> To hire his death so."

But Jonson as the professional exploiter of human follies is naturally even more concerned with the quack and the magician. The latter, indeed, if we are to accept comedy as an image of the times, found himself more on the road to preferment than the legitimate physician.

"He's a rare physician, do him right," says Sir Epicure Mammon,

> "An excellent Paracelsian, and has done
> Strange cures with mineral physic. He deals all

With spirits, he; He will not hear a word
Of Galen, or his tedious recipes."

Similarly, Marlowe's Faustus, although through
his prescriptions whole cities have already

"Escaped the plague
And thousand desperate maladies been eased,"

feels that he is still "but Faustus and a man". If
"this profession were to be esteemed", then must
the physician turn magician, and legitimate thera-
peutics give place to miracles.

It would almost seem, indeed, that the emphasis
of the professional medical man upon incantations
and natural magic left the field of legitimate heal-
ing open to the heroines of romance. "For I tell
thee, Tristan, this wound shall be thy death, for
the sword was poisoned with a deadly poison, and
no leech nor leechcraft can heal thee, saving only
my sister Iseult, the Queen of Ireland. She knoweth
the virtues of all plants, and many secrets of heal-
ing; she can heal thee, but none other on earth
can."

Nor were the fictitious royalties of romance the
only rivals of the doctors: for it will be remembered
that the English kings healed for the "King's evil"
from the days of Edward the Confessor to the time
when Queen Anne "touched" the future great cham
of literature, Samuel Johnson.

Meanwhile the devotees of surgery, to whom the

privileges of magic were denied, eked out their practice with humbler expedients. In the medical schools of the middle ages the actual handling of surgery was frequently relegated to the village barber, who was usually village dentist and village musician as well. The teeth which he had drawn were not infrequently hung up at the window on lute-strings; the parti-coloured barber's pole was painted after the fashion of a surgeon's bandage, and outside of the door, to indicate his double function of barber and surgeon, hung "a copper basin on a prickant spear." "Yonder his mansion is," says Mine Host in *The Knight of the Burning Pestle,* as he directs Ralph to the den of the "giant Barbaroso";

> "Lo, where the spear and copper basin are!
> Behold that string on which hangs many a tooth
> Drawn from the gentle jaw of wandering
>   knights."

The cutbeards of Elizabethan drama are ready alike with razor, scalpel, or physic, and are also the stock intermediaries of intrigue. Even in the eighteenth century, medicine had strange bed-fellows. Partridge, the almanac-maker, who describes himself as an "honest physician," was a cobbler by trade, and is characterized, in a pamphlet written in his behalf, as "an eminent practitioner in leather, physic, and astrology."

The eighteenth century with its fresh heritage

from the great discovery of Harvey, with such men
as Sydenham and Sir Thomas Browne to look back
to, and with its own Arbuthnots, and Garths, and
Akensides handing on the medical tradition of
honourable accomplishment in letters, might well
have portrayed the physician with respect in its
creative literature; but comedy found the burlesque
doctor made to its hand by Molière, accepted the
stage quack as unquestioningly as it had already
accepted the *miles gloriosus,* and in such comedies
as Fielding's *Mock Doctor,* and Cobb's *Doctor and
Apothecary,* out-Molière'd the master in *facetiæ*
at the physician's expense; and prose fiction contented itself with the Dr. Slops, the Partridges, and
the low quacks and imposters who infest the pages
of Smollett.

Satirical and burlesque pictures of the physician
abound in nineteenth century fiction; but Charles
Reade is the only one who seems, like Molière, to
have singled them out as the special object of male-
volence. His portraits are too long for transcrip-
tion, but the phrases in which he hits off the foibles
of the profession are often neatly turned and quot-
able,—as in his characterization of one doctor as
a "mellifluous pleonast, who oiled his prescriptions
with fresh polysyllables." In the novels of Dickens
the general practitioner, even when he assumes the
venerable dignity of Doctor Manette in *The Tale
of Two Cities,* carries his profession only as a sort
of shadowy accessory. I fancy more than one

physician in reading the novel must have smiled at
the idea that Doctor Manette, after being rescued,
aged and mentally clouded, from the oblivion of
the Bastille, should have been able to "earn as
much as he wanted" by the practice of his profession. The surgeon, on the other hand, usually
brings his profession with him into the centre of
the stage, but he remains a sawbones, a comic and
usually disreputable figure, of whom Bob Sawyer
may stand as typical.

It is not surprising that in Dickens, with his vast
canvases, physicians are fairly numerous; but in
Thackeray medicine is almost completely crowded
out by the other two learned professions. One is
inclined to wonder a bit at this, too, for several of
Thackeray's warmest friendships were with physicians, to one of whom *Pendennis* is dedicated in
words which glow with the gratitude of a conval-
escent recently rescued from death. And yet the
practitioner in the pages of Thackeray concerning
whom the present writer at least has the most lively
memories, is one from the pages of that very novel,
one who was most anxious to bury his professional
past in oblivion, and be addressed not as Doctor,
but as Squire. And this ancestral Pendennis, ex-
apothecary, ex-doctor, conveniently sketched in
with the kindly condescension which Thackeray
sometimes allowed himself, and quite forgotten
when the author gets down to the serious business
of the novel, is typical of the other physicians in

Thackeray. Some of them, it is true, are on a much more assured social footing than the former dispenser of salts and plasters, but all of them are there only to serve their casual turn, and the author has other game afoot than to develop these occasional functionaries into finished portraits.

Of the great Victorian novelists, it remained for George Eliot to give the profession a central place in one of her novels, and to produce a character which would be convincing alike to the physician and the layman. Lydgate, says Dr. S. Weir Mitchell, "is all over the physician, his manner, his sentiments, his modes of thought, but he stands alone in fiction." Lydgate is a wonderful picture, not merely because his idealism and devotion, under adverse conditions, to the literature of his profession strike a responsive chord in the breast of such a physician as Dr. Mitchell, but because these traits are so melted into Lydgate's daily life that they are the man; and the study of his degeneration is precisely the study of the deterioration of his professional self under a barren and unsympathetic environment.

More recent fiction has been productive of many studies of the profession, such as Miss Jewett's *The Country Doctor,* and W. D. Howells' *Dr. Breen's Practice.* The last decade or two has seen also the emergence of the woman-physician as a type in fiction, but there has been nothing so comprehensive or so convincing as Lydgate since

Middlemarch came from the press. When some novelist appears worthy to take up the pen which George Eliot laid down, an opportunity awaits him in a territory through which Kipling has blazed the way in *Marklake Witches,*—the presentation in fiction of some of the great physicians of former times, in the full stress of their epochal lives. What a "story" there would be, for example, in the career of Harvey, son of Kentish yeoman, adviser and physician of royalty, standing in the transition moment between ancient and modern medicine, declaring his discovery of the circulation of the blood in words that have not lost their fine ring throughout the centuries:

"But what remains to be said upon the quantity and source of the blood which thus passes, is of a character so novel and unheard of that I not only fear injury to myself from the envy of a few, but I tremble lest I have mankind at large for my enemies, so much doth wont and custom become a second nature. Doctrine once sown strikes deep its root, and respect for antiquity influences all men. Still the die is cast, and my trust is in my love of truth and the candour of cultivated minds."

How the historical imagination, like a highly sensitized plate, could catch and register the receding faces of that throng of sixteenth century quacks and impostors, panderers to the ancient mystery of medicine, as they peer over the line drawn by this demonstrator of the fundamental principle on which all modern knowledge of the human body rests! And with what heightened satisfaction would the reader of such a story detect in the literature of Harvey's own day the ferment of interest on the subject, which could induce the poet Donne, for example, to introduce into one of his elegiac poems the query:

"Know'st thou how blood, which to the heart
    doth flow,
Doth from one ventricle to the other go?"

or encourage Harvey's fellow-Kentishman and fellow-Cambridge student, Phineas Fletcher, to make the conception of the human body as an island bounded by streams of blood the theme of the long Spenserian poem, "The Purple Island"!

Or what a theme in Jenner's discovery of vaccination, with all the superstitious follies of the riotous crowds, who opposed a blessing so disguised; and with poor little eight-year old James Phipps preserved to history as the first subject of experiment!

And what possibilities for historical fiction, too, in some of the men whom a more ephemeral brilliance has kept in memory—Arbuthnot and his circle of wits and literary geniuses; Heberden, Dr. Johnson's *Ultimus Romanorum*; Dr. John Brown, of Edinburgh, the author of the one-time famous "Brunonian theory"; or that other Dr. John Brown to whom the world is indebted for *Rab and His*

Friends; or Mark Akenside, butcher's son, poet, and physician, distinguished alike for the richness of his language and the meanness of his character, and pilloried in the pages of *Peregrine Pickle*.

Studies such as these would go far towards recompensing medicine for the scurvy treatment which literature has been disposed to accord it; but the debt of literature to medicine is too various to be readily repaid. Not the least of these obligations is the matter of vocabulary.

The essence of literature has always been the analysis and interpretation of character; and English literature, prior to the seventeenth century, borrowed from contemporary medicine a mode of thought and a system of terminology which became the universal literary language of characterization. The doctrine of humours, blood, phlegm, choler (or yellow bile) and melancholy (or black bile) creating a temperament sanguine, phlegmatic, choleric or melancholy, established itself in English poetry from Chaucer to Milton as the regular means of portrayal of disposition, temperament, and mood, and through its transitional sense of *caprice* gave us *humour* in its present significance. In the eighteenth century, the melancholy humour of Shakespeare's day gave place to the spleen—a general medico-literary term for the vapours, the blues—in short, for all those combinations of physical and mental discomfort which proceed from a disordered stomach and a perverted imagination. Pope's picture of the Cave of Spleen, where the Goddess

". . . Sighs forever on her pensive bed,
     Pain at her side and Megrim at her head,"

is properly balanced with Matthew Green's famous prescription for the cure of the disease—

"Fling but a stone, the giant dies.
     Laugh and be well."

Or again, the word "nerve", after supplying the sixteenth and seventeenth centuries with the adjective nervous, meaning sinewy, and the eighteenth and nineteenth centuries with the same adjective, meaning easily excitable, and therefore weak, has completed the cycle by becoming the modern slang synonym for impertinence.

Meanwhile, through the crystallization of metaphors, we retain memorials of the ancient fallacies concerning the human body. "My reins", it is said in Proverbs, "shall rejoice when thy lips speak right things." "Thou thing of no bowels," says Thersites to Ajax in Shakespeare's *Troilus and Cressida*. "Joseph made haste", we are told in Genesis, "for his bowels did yearn upon his brother"; and we find the quaint and witty divine, Thomas Fuller, describing "Bloody Bonner, that corpulent tyrant" as "full of guts but empty of bowels". We still "learn by heart", though science has long since

given over the idea that the heart is the seat of
memory. The same organ rests secure as the seat
of passion, though in Elizabethan times the liver
vied with it. I think that it is in one of Beaumont
and Fletcher's plays that a lover complains to his
unresponsive mistress: "You have no liver".
Orsino, in *Twelfth Night*, reprehending the inadequacy of women's love, accuses them of having "no
motion of the liver". Elizabethan literature is
full of such examples.

"What authority we have", says Elia, "in history
or mythology for placing the headquarters and
metropolis of god Cupid in this anatomical seat
(the heart) rather than in any other is not very
clear; but we have got it, and it will serve as well
as any other. Else we might easily imagine, upon
some other system which might have prevailed for
anything which our pathology knows to the contrary, a lover addressing his mistress, in perfect
simplicity of feeling, 'Madam, my *liver* and for-
tunes are entirely at your disposal', or putting a
delicate question, 'Amanda, have you a midriff to
bestow?' But custom has settled these things, and
awarded the seat of sentiment to the aforesaid
triangle, while its less fortunate neighbours wait
at animal and anatomical distance."

The Elizabethan, John Lyly, summed up a whole
anatomy of misfits in a single sentence:

"How say you, Favilla, is not love a lurcher
(thief) that taketh men's stomachs away that they

cannot eat, their spleen that they cannot laugh, their hearts that they cannot fight, their eyes that they cannot sleep, and leaveth nothing but livers to make nothing but lovers?"

But if English literature has incurred chance obligations in the way of borrowings from the vocabulary of the doctors, it is under a far more considerable obligation to the direct literary contributions of the doctors themselves. From generation to generation the profession has included many who, like John Brown's ideal physician, "live in the world of letters as a freeholder," and believe that "their profession and their patients need not suffer, though their *horæ subsecivæ* are devoted occasionally to miscellaneous thinking and reading." The achievements of these men are too comprehensive to be dealt with in this brief compass, and too familiar indeed to require more than mention; but it is worth while to remember at least that Thomas Linacre, one of the great classical scholars and leaders of the English Renaissance, was physician to Henry VIII; that Lodge, the Elizabethan novelist and poet, spent the latter part of his life in the practice of medicine; that Locke, author of the *Essay concerning the Human Understanding,* was a physician and practised privately; that some of the noblest and most eloquent prose in the language has been left to us by a physician, Sir Thomas Browne; that Garth and Akenside and Arbuthnot wrote notably in their day; that one of the best

novels, two of the best comedies, and some of the
best poetry in the eighteenth century, were written
by the physician, Oliver Goldsmith; that one of the
most prolific and vigorous novelists of the eighteenth century, Tobias Smollett, practised medicine; that one of the most beautiful and enduring
of all short stories, *Rab and His Friends,* was written by a physician, Dr. John Brown; that poets as
diverse as Crabbe and Keats emerged from the
study of medicine into the worship of the Muse;
that a physician—and one of the leaders of his profession—Dr. Oliver Wendell Holmes, endeared
himself wherever the English language is spoken,
by the grace and sympathetic humour of his poetry
and essays; that one of the most successful novelists of yesterday was the noted physician, Dr. S.
Weir Mitchell; and that no man among recent
writers had a more practised pen and a purer style
than the master-physician, Sir William Osler.

Of all these men, who have contributed with
varying degrees of distinction to English literature,
it is curious to observe that Dr. Holmes alone, so
to speak, superimposed his vocation upon his avo-
cation, and kept us constantly reminded that it
was a medical man who held the pen.   Browne
loved to drift into an *O Altitudo,* where the mate-
rialities of medicine would have been out of place;
Goldsmith never seemed to care enough about his
profession to make literary capital of it; but Holmes
fashioned his medical knowledge into prose fiction,

into essays, into poetry—and fashioned it so deftly that his works constitute the immortal meeting-ground of medicine and English literature. "The universe swam in an ocean of similitudes and analogies" for Dr. Holmes; and if it was the pathologist who wrote *Elsie Venner*, it was the biologist who coined the similitude of the "Chambered Nautilus." What, moreover, could surpass the delightful effrontery of that passage in the *Autocrat*, where the doctor discovers that the young lady is in love because her breathing becomes *thoracic*, or that other where the aspirations and passions of his youth become confused in mellow reminiscence with his first dabblings in chemistry —"orange-coloured fumes of nitrous acid and visions as bright and transient; reddening litmus-paper and blushing cheeks;—*eheu!*

'Soles occidere et redire possunt!'

but there is no reagent that will redden the faded roses of eighteen hundred and——"

There was a moment in the closing years of Dr. Holmes's life when he was compelled to balance these two things, his medical achievements and his literary creation, over against each other. It was Dr. Osler who forced the issue by writing a letter to Dr. Holmes, asking which he valued more, "the 'Essay on Puerperal Fever,' which had saved many lives, or the 'Chambered Nautilus' which had given pleasure to so many thousands."

"I think I will not answer the question you put me," wrote Dr. Holmes in reply. "I had a savage pleasure, I confess, in handling those two professors. . . . But in writing the poem, I was filled with a better feeling—the highest state of mental exaltation and the most crystalline clairvoyance, as it seemed to me, that had ever been granted to me. . . . There is more selfish pleasure to be had out of the poem—perhaps a nobler satisfaction from the life-saving labour."

So spoke the innate modesty which always went hand in hand with the good doctor's frank liking for the things that were his. Explicitly the question remained unanswered, but who shall say that the soul of the doctor did not answer it as we should have done, or that the scales fluctuated long when medicine and literature were thus weighed in the balance?

*   *   *   *

This was an *entree*—or perhaps rather, a salad—which the Canadian Medical Association benevolently introduced into the meaty menu of one of their annual meetings many years ago. If it were to do over, now, I think that I should substitute for most of these casual notes a comparative study of two books: Sinclair Lewis' *Arrowsmith* and Axel Munthe's *San Michele*. What a contrast—in background, in matter, in manner, in artistry! But if one should dig down beneath the superficial differences to the underlying strain of professional idealism, what a grand time one would have showing that Judy O'Grady and the Colonel's lady were sisters under their skins!

But it is just as well for me, perhaps, that neither book was written then; for this would be a job for a doctor-philosopher, not a mere man of letters.

TIME O' DAY ON PARNASSUS

T HIS is not an essay, Gentle Reader. It is only
a sheaf of quotations, bound together with the
cord of the passing hours—but it is much better
than any essay of mine, for the quotations are
excellent ones. And familiar though they be to you,
you will, I promise, find renewed pleasure in them
here, for the sake of the cord which binds them.

I had been reading Chaucer's treatise on the
Astrolabe and possibly had not apprehended
"verray perfitly" the nature of that noble instrument, which Chaucer was so gravely expounding to
his "litel Lowis". At any rate, time had rather
ambled with me, until I reached the words: "And
in this wyse hadde I the experience for ever-mo in
which maner I sholde knowe the tyd of the day. . . .
Among an heep of sterris fixe, it lyked me for to
take the altitude of the feire white sterre that is
cleped Alhabor." The quaint words set me adrift
in a mood of dreamy speculation, evoked by
Chaucer's "feire white sterre" and the "tyd of day"
which it lyked him to find. Is there not for every
poet a tyd of the day which best lyketh him, and
is there not in our horologe of dreams a poet for
each passing hour?

As for the father of "litel Lowis", was he not in

all senses the "Morning Star" of English poetry?
We should brook it ill were his mood other than
the dawn of our diurnal round.

> "As I seyde erst, whan comen is the May
> Than in my bed ther daweth me no day
> That I nam up and walking in the mede."

And is it not true in general that it is only the more
robust poets who have minted this matutinal glory
of the sun into the fine gold of their song?   At the
moment when

> ". . . the morn in russet mantle clad
> Walks o'er the dew of yon high eastward hill"

and the lark sings at heaven's gate, then rise too
our hearty singers, the hierarchy of lusty bards
whose blood is quickened with the new day.   Let
the decadents sing of the mild moonlight or the cold
stars; we shall choir the moment when

> "Aurora throws her fair
> Fresh quilted colours through the air."

*   *   *   *   *

> "When all the birds have matins said
> And sung their thankful hymns, 'tis sin,
> Nay, profanation, to stay in."

Not for us the delicate *nuances* of the dawn; but

> "Faster and more fast

O'er night's brim day boils at last:
Boils, pure gold, o'er the cloud-cup's brim
Where spurting and suppressed it lay
For not a frothflake touched the rim
Of yonder gap in the solid gray
Of the eastern cloud, an hour away;
But forth one wavelet, then another curled
Till the whole sunrise, not to be suppressed,
Rose, reddened, and its seething breast
Flickered in bounds, grew gold, then
    overflowed the world."

Nor is it only the glory of May-time matins to which Stout Heart responds. Proper joyance too, he finds, in the

"Good gigantic smile o' the brown old earth
This autumn morning! How he sets his bones
To bask i' the sun, and thrusts out knees and
    feet
For the ripple to run over in its mirth!"

But if the matutinal sunlight stirs the blood and rouses the lusty poet to his joy, the passive noon-tide, moment of rich rest after labour, evokes a singer of spirit less robust. Not now the thrill of the pulses with which Chaucer or Shakespeare or Herrick or Browning throws himself into the light that overflows a world. Rather shall we share with Tennyson the plentitude of the moment when

". . . noonday quiet holds the hill;
The grasshopper is silent in the grass;

The lizard, with his shadow on the stone
Rests like a shadow, and the winds are dead."

or live again with Theocritus that noontide of the
opulent Sicilian summer when "on shadowy boughs
the burnt cicalas kept their chattering toil, far off
the little owl cried in the thick thorn brake, the
larks and finches were singing, the ring dove
moaned and the yellow bees were flitting about the
springs."

The meridian passes and with it the morning
vigour and the noontide bliss. The poet of the
waning day is of a more reflective mood.

"Yet will I temperately rejoice;
Wide is the range and free the choice
Of undiscordant themes
Which haply kindred souls may prize
Not less than vernal ecstasies
And passion's feverish dreams."

With him,

". . . with an eye made quiet by the power
Of harmony, and the deep power of joy,
We see into the life of things."

While

"The sun above the mountain's head,
A freshening lustre mellow,
Through all the long green fields has spread
His first sweet evening yellow."

But "the golden close of evening" melts into twi-

light. The clear outlines and perfect definition of
the day blur into the mysterious shadows of the
coming night. This boding presence, akin to the
solemn fact of Death, summons a poet of finer
essence—

> ". . . a poet hidden
>   In the light of thought,
>   Singing hymns unbidden,
>   Till the world is wrought
> To sympathy with hopes and fears it heeded
>   not:"

For thy coming, Spirit of the Night

> "Out of the misty eastern cave
>   Where, all the long and lone daylight
>   Thou wovest dreams of joy and fear,
>   Which make thee terrible and dear,—"

for thy coming has he waited—

> "When I arose and saw the dawn,
>   I sighed for thee;
>   When light rode high, and the dew was gone;
>   And noon lay heavy on flower and tree,
>   And the weary Day turned to his rest,
>   Lingering like an unloved guest,
>   I sighed for thee.

> "Thy brother Death came, and cried,
>   Wouldst thou me?
>   Thy sweet child Sleep, the filmy-eyed,
>   Murmured like a noon-tide bee,
>   Shall I nestle near thy side?

Wouldst thou me?—And I replied,
   No, not thee!

"Death will come when thou art dead,
   Soon, too soon—
Sleep will come when thou art fled;
Of neither would I ask the boon
I ask of thee, belovèd Night—
Swift be thine approaching flight,
   Come soon, soon!"

And the coming night, shall it be moonlight or starlight? In the choice of a poet for other periods of our diurnal round, there may be room for diversity of opinion; but for moonlight there is one poet and for starlight there is one poet—one poet and no more.

For now we cast off melancholy in the presence of

"The coy moon, when in the waviness
Of whitest clouds she does her beauty dress,
And staidly paces higher up and higher
Like a sweet nun in holiday attire."

Or in a more impassioned mood we hark to Endymion what time he

"Saw emerge
The loveliest moon that ever silver'd o'er
A shell for Neptune's goblet; she did soar
So passionately bright, my dazzled soul,
Commingling with her argent spheres did roll

Through clear and cloudy, even when she went
At last into a dark and vapoury tent—
Whereat, methought, the lidless-eyèd train
Of planets all were in the blue again."

But when the moon has vanished and left the
night to the silent dominion of the stars, or when,
on a night unvisited by the wandering moon, we
see

"On the pure horizon far
Pulsing with the first-born star
The liquid sky above the hill.
The evening comes, the fields are still—"

for this moment and for all the starlit night there
is no voice save the voice of Matthew Arnold. For
him, the stars are not merely a beauty of the night,
they are the key to his soul.

"Unaffrighted by the silence round them,
Undistracted by the sights they see,
These demand not that the things without
them
Yield them love, amusement, sympathy."

* * * * *

"For self-poised they live, nor pine with noting
All the fever of some differing soul."

Amid the pettiness and vanity of the dwellers on
the plain,

"The solemn peaks but to the stars are known."

The thoughts of one whose faith is strong

"Rain their steady glow
Like stars on life's cold sea";

and death is

"The long night whose stillness brooks no star."

But the stars grow pale as the east lightens with
the promise of another day. The cycle of the hours
is complete and the solemn meditation of the starlit night is dissipated with the first rays of the
returning sun. Let not our memories be other than
bright, for we have drunk together of the cup of
remembered beauty, sweet as the honey of Hymet-
tus. We hearken to the voice of the goatherd in
Theocritus: "Lo, here is thy cup, see, my friend,
of how pleasant a savour. Thou wilt think it has
been dipped in the well-spring of the Hours."

THE PLOT MACHINE: OR, HAMLET UP TO DATE

L EST you suspect me of making it up, I hasten to explain that the letter came from Los Angeles. As a conventionally-minded member of a credible world, I couldn't have made it up. The idea simply wouldn't have occurred to me. The document lies before me. I can produce it on demand.

The writer of the letter is evidently a friend of a friend of mine. Toward the friends of his friend, his heart is warm.

"Dear Friend", he begins, "An editor friend of yours"—what a pleasure to learn that I have an editor friend in Los Angeles!—"an editor friend of yours suggests that we mail you information concerning the Plot Machine—or Martin Luther Higginbotham's Plot-Robot, as it has been called in hundreds of newspaper and magazine articles. So—here it is!

"One well-known author—within 60 days after purchasing the Plot Machine—writes us that he has sold two short stories, a human-interest article, and a 30,000-word novelette, all plotted with its aid. The editor of a group of twelve national magazines, after reviewing the Plot Machine, requested that literature be sent to all his contributing authors. We have scores of enthusiastic endorsements from authors everywhere, who testify to the superior merits of this new tool for writers. . . . By charting a definite course for the imagination and supplying the necessary material, it will provide outlines for millions of novel and refreshing plots.

"The Plot Machine will quickly build a plot structure around any idea—character—*locale*—situation—or combination of these which one may have in mind. Its ability to 'pep up' the plots of rejected stories is really marvellous! . . . ."

From this friendly letter, which concludes with a flattering suggestion that as a "recognized author" I would find the Plot Machine most helpful, I turned with avidity to the printed circular. There I found that "with every nine turns of the disc", the Plot Machine would supply my "creative imagination" with "a complete story plot structure"; and that it would put my will "in absolute control of its tremendous creative powers" so that I could "quickly make it produce any kind of plot" that I desired—"and *very* quickly too!" "As it divorces ideas which have been associated together in so many yarns, creating new affinities, it will not develop a hackneyed plot or one with loose ends, blind alleys and devoid of suspense. Every Plot Machine plot is a PERFECT PLOT."

I had never attempted a short story, or a human-interest article or a 30,000 word novelette; but when I learned that the Plot Machine could supply "sixty-four thousand eight hundred love affairs—one thousand and eighty human problems—every possible obstacle to love, dramatic complication, predicament, crisis and climax", the world lay all before me where to choose. Why should I continue to teach the young idea how to shoot, when with nine turns of the disc I could do my own shooting? Obviously there was nothing for it but to dig up ten dollars to-morrow morning and order the Plot Machine. What if I did have to borrow my wife's pin money? One 30,000 word novelette with the cinema rights ("We might say that we have established a very desirable connection of the kind which assures prompt and favourable consideration of meritorious material") and she could deck herself

> "With silken coats and caps and golden rings,
> With ruffs and cuffs and farthingales and
>   things;
> With scarfs and fans and double change of
>   bravery."

But the hour waxed late and I went to sleep. Whether it was then or toward the waking hour of the morning I do not know; but I fancy that pretty well throughout the night that disc must have been turning in my head. Sometime, at any rate, I became conscious that *Hamlet* was a hackneyed plot even when Shakespeare appropriated it, and that, as my Los Angeles editor friend would have said, it had been getting hackneyeder and hackneyeder ever since. Nine times I turned the disc. Formless space materialized into a stage, and from the wings,

with an effect slightly phantasmagoric, but none
the less comforting, beamed the dear-friendly
countenance of Martin Luther Higginbotham.
"That ghost-stuff don't go any more," he explained.
"Lets the cat out of the bag right at the beginning,
too. What's the sense of knowing, bang off, who
killed old Hamlet, and then us listenin' for two
mortal hours to young Hamlet just kiddin' himself along, and then having Claudius kick the
bucket as you might say mostly by accident?"

Just here I found myself beginning to harbour a
sneaking respect for Martin L. How many times
had I said in the class-room: "Read independently,
young men. Nothing is sacrosanct. Have the
courage of your convictions!" But who among
them had ever read *Hamlet* as independently as
that?

Martin L. Higginbotham's voice boomed on;
and as it boomed the stage became the authentic
castle of Elsinore and glittering figures surrounded
a table in a stately banquet hall. "What gets me",
said Mr. Higginbotham, "is how Bill Shakespeare
missed so many chances. Nothing starts a play off
like a good hot drinking-scene. There was Shakespeare mouthing about how Claudius drained his
draughts of Rhenish down,—and actually old W.
S. didn't have the sense to stage it and let the crowd
see Claudius get tight. "Now *that*", said Mr.
Higginbotham, as Claudius executed a demi-volte

and slid under the table—"now *that* is the way it
ought to have begun."

"But where's Hamlet?" I feebly enquired.

"Oh, Hamlet," said Mr. Higginbotham, "he isn't
back yet. He's still away at the great Mid-western
university of Wittenbunk. He's crack pitcher on
the Varsity baseball team and when the home-
folks wired him that his father had passed on, he
simply *couldn't* let the fellows down by leaving just
before the big game. But *that's* all right. He's
been taking special courses in Path-Psy and De-
Fic;* he's just about to get back, and in the next
scene you'll see him make things hum.

"Yes," said Mr. Higginbotham, as the stage became the throne-room and Claudius and Gertrude
and the courtiers waited expectantly, "Yes, of
course Hamlet guessed from the start that there
was something rotten in the state of Denmark.
He'd wired old Polonius when the news came to
arrange a private post-mortem and when Hamlet
got back I'll say that Polonius gave him an ear-full.
Hamlet had suspected Claudius right along as an
interested party, but how was he to get the goods
on him? As for Polonius, you can bet your bottom
dollar he hadn't spilled the post-mortem. Not he.
Curious how people have misunderstood Polonius.
What had he been Chamberlain all those years for
if he hadn't learned the trick of talking in circles
and saying nothing? Not a word, Sir, till Hamlet
got back. And then between them they cooked

---

*A letter from the Registrar of Wittenbunk informs me
that these abbreviations stand for Pathological Psychology and
Detective Fiction.

it up that Hamlet would act daffy and Polonius go round saying that Hamlet had cracked because Ophelia had turned him down. Pretty good detective work, I'll tell the world. Time was what they wanted—and a free hand.

"Hamlet *kill* Polonius? Not on your life, Sir; not in *my* version. That was just another one of Bill Shakespeare's mistakes. A pair of schemers, those two were. And they are going to be in cahoots from start to finish.

"Watch this scene. Bill was really on the job here and I didn't need to do a thing but tone down the high brow poetry and pep up the Player-King. See Claudius about to do a skedaddle. White as a sheet he is, and scared stiff. There he goes! Hamlet has something on him now,—but not enough, not enough. The King might say he'd just had a fit or something. Anyway, Hamlet's too cool a customer to be in a rush, and that course in De-Fic has taught him a thing or two.

"What am I going to do about Hamlet's catching the King at prayer? Why, cut it out, of course! If ever there was a piece of plain bunk, that was it. Who ever heard of anybody thinking out loud for ten minutes, and spilling his most secret thoughts to the whole audience? A convention of the stage, you say? Hamlet couldn't hear him? Well, Hamlet was standing right behind him, wasn't he? The trouble with so much of Shakespeare is that it won't wash. And that business about the King's having a fifty-fifty chance of going to heaven if he were killed on his knees. Do you think that would have stopped Hamlet if he'd been all set? But he wasn't. It was more proof he needed—*and* witnesses.

"The scene where Hamlet tries to make Gertrude come across? Yes, we'll have that. Of course Hamlet is going to cross-examine everybody who might have had a hand in it. There it goes. Gertrude is some flustered. But after all, Hamlet has a soft spot for the old lady. That guy, Claudius, was a hypnotist. Hamlet had studied that in Path-Psy. You couldn't blame Gertrude—and anyway she wasn't onto Claudius's game.

"Well, just here the plot gets kinder complicated. Laertes gets back from somewhere-or-other, and muscles in. Ophelia was really in love with Hamlet and when he turns her down she drowns herself. We'll cut out her silly songs but stage a drowning scene with a tank of real water. Just watch her do it! And then Laertes gets back and hears all about it, and fights Hamlet in her grave. That's a wow. Hamlet knocks him out in one round—biff, on the solar plexus. There's no more fight in Laertes—and now the coast is clear for Hamlet and Polonius to get in their detective work.

"The point that foxy old Polonius has been working on all the while is that Claudius is a poison-specialist. Do you remember the "leperous distilment"? Well, ever since the post-mortem showed that old Hamlet had been poisoned, Polonius had been working on that. It was gin, Sir, made with wood-alcohol, that had done for old Hamlet. And Polonius, who had been snooping around all this while, had located the still. Polonius had got the goods on Claudius, and all Polonius and Hamlet needed was somebody to put it up to. And then Fortinbras happened along. They weren't very particular about the how-come of judges in those days. Remember how Portia just sorter turned up in Venice when Antonio was on trial? Well, Fortinbras turns up, and they put it up to him. There they are in the throne-room once more. Only there's nobody on the throne. They've got Claudius in a box with a couple of Fortinbras' he-men to guard him. And here come Rosencrantz and Guildenstern. Claudius had hired them to spy on Hamlet, but Hamlet slipped 'em a grand apiece, and they've been spying on Claudius instead. They were listening behind the arras when Claudius put it up to Laertes to fence with Hamlet. One of the foils would be poisoned, but the best bet would be another drink of Claudius' gin that they'd give Hamlet just before the match. Hamlet got in ahead and the fencing-match didn't come off—but now Rosencrantz and Guildenstern are spilling the whole thing at the trial.

"No chance for appeals and legal trickery in those days. Fortinbras is short and sharp. 'Stand him up against that wall,' says Fortinbras, pointing at Claudius. 'Hamlet, you've got a gun. Well, use it, and be quick about it.'

" 'Now, you fellows,' says Fortinbras, 'I've got a date in Poland, and I'm in a hurry. Hamlet is next heir. Set him on the throne, and that's that.' "

B-r-r-r-r, goes the alarm-bell. Morning again —and I have a lecture at 9.30. Same old stuff. "Read independently, young men. Nothing is sacrosanct. Have the courage of your convictions." But the drudgery will be over soon. Nine turns of the disc. . . . .

GENIUS AT SCHOOL

TO THE average man there is something peculiarly daunting in the precocity of literary genius. Pope, lisping in numbers; Charlotte Brontë, at fourteen classifying her twenty-two manuscript volumes of "works"; Elizabeth Barrett, writing an epic when she was eleven; Macaulay, composing at seven an epitome of universal history—what can the ordinary man make of such superhuman infants?

And when the ordinary man is a school teacher by profession, and has served in the cause of all the muses (except Terpsichore) for longer than ever Jacob served for Rachel, and always in the hope that he might catch a genius young, these precocious beings assume a kind of remoteness, a quality of unreality. They must have existed. Their works do follow them; the glowing pages of E.M.L. and the dogged statistics of D.N.B. equally attest their actuality; but neither the intuition of the moment, nor the retrospective wisdom which comes to the teacher when John and James and Henry have passed out of his immediate vision and made careers for themselves, has ever won for him a single glimpse through this east window of divine surprise.

Will it ever come, one wonders. And if it does, what on earth would one do? Would one help or hinder? Nay, rather, would one know? Ah, there's the rub. How many apparent geniuses has not the teacher seen rise through all the gradations of academic success, until in cap and gown, they mounted the rostrum and pronounced the well earned and well turned lines of the valedictory!

"Up the pinnacled glory reached and the pride of my soul was in sight."

And then oblivion marked them for its own, and slowly disillusionment came to the eager teacher. Not discontent, for the work had always been worth doing, and worth enjoying; but at least so much of disillusionment as belonged to the discovery that academic attainment had not led and possibly never would lead him to that east window.

Moreover, the teacher remembered that long ago, he too had been the valedictorian of his year. He recalled the sea of faces in the great auditorium on commencement day, his gasping fear as he advanced to the front of the stage that he would forget the well conned lines of his valedictory, the glow that suffused him as he got his grip again, and the way in which the audience hung upon his words. Did he not know himself to be a genius then? And in the growing wisdom of years, has he not seen the spark fade until he could not revive it, however much he blew upon the dimming embers? "He who can, does"; says the cynical Mr. Shaw. "He who cannot, teaches."

No, academic attainment is not a certain way.

He is proud of his good students, but he has not seen them become geniuses, and he is not so sure of his prize-winners as he used to be. How then shall he know? These real geniuses of the past once went to school, and some forgotten school-master hugged the memory of them to his breast in his old age. May it not be that one will emerge even in this far corner of the Northwest? Stranger things have happened. But if he comes, will he seem only a queer erratic little fellow, hovering uneasily on the verge of the orderly routine? Will he remain

> ". . . . hidden
> In the light of thought
> Singing hymns unbidden"?

Or shall his teacher, even he, surprise that young poetic soul into shy confidences and catch a moment's precious vision of the time when the world shall be

> ". . . . wrought
> To sympathy with hopes and fears it heeded
> not"?

But this is the stuff that dreams are made of. Every year has had its confessions, but so far there has been no hint of the east window. Meanwhile, leaving such happy chances in the lap of the gods, can one not find a standard qualification or two, an acid-test, to recognize the budding genius by? "You defined genius," says J. R. Green in one of his letters, "as a peculiar aptitude for a certain branch of study. Pardon me, that is talent. Genius is a much higher thing: the power of bending circumstances to our will". That ought to do. These academic circumstances which pass into the currency of education as courses and lessons—how zealously young Artful Dodger bends them to his will! Herbert Spencer records in his autobiography that, at nine years of age, he "rejected Latin grammar because of its lack of system." Now the determined rejection of Latin Grammar at a comparatively tender age ought to establish a reasonable presumption that one has discovered a young Herbert Spencer. And when one reads farther the same philosopher's confession: "If ever I said a lesson correctly, it was very rarely," one really begins to believe that the evidence is accumulating.

And then there was Henry Thomas Buckle. The one thing which Buckle wanted was to escape the thraldom of a formal education. He did not like mathematics. His father offered him any reward he might name, if he would win the medal in that subject. The boy won it, and named as his reward —to be taken away from school. The teacher has never seen the thing accomplished in just that way in his own experience, but he has seen as much intelligence and systematic effort expended with a similar object, on more than one occasion. He knew a boy once who acted as the presiding genius (in both senses) of the court of how not to do it, during all the four years of his academic career, and whose right to that high office became a veritable tradition in after years. The teacher did not recognize this quality as a hall mark of genius at the time; but that boy has come nearer since to displaying the true quality of creative genius than any other person who ever fell under the teacher's personal observation.

The good obstinate rejecter! It is at least an encouragingly tangible type. The teacher is watching them, and he may catch a real genius among them some day.

And then there are the lazy ones—that ever present horde of genial ne'er-do-wells who of the pleasant art of shirking have made a vocation, and who will labour at it even as Falstaff did at purse-taking—

"Why, Hal, 'tis my vocation, Hal. 'Tis no sin for a man to labour in his vocation."

In his younger days the teacher found them irritating, and warned them of the wrath to come. But as he grew in years and in knowledge of the past, he learned that even in such lowly tenements genius sometimes hath its seat. And while he spurred them no less zealously to their work, he grew to threaten them less and to scorn them not at all. He remembered the beloved Stevenson, "pattern of an idler . . . with infinite yawning during lecture and unquenchable gusto in the delights of truantry"; and glorious Sir Walter, "incorrigibly idle imp" at school, who loved to tell of how at the University Professor Dalzell "pronounced upon me the severe sentence that dunce I was and dunce was to remain."

And when these same amiable idlers had loitered along the pleasant bypaths of an education until they were like to become a permanent part of the college landscape, and by dint of passing an easy course here, and being boosted by eleventh-hour crammers through a hard course there, had at last "come up" for a degree, the teacher again found his attitude changing with the years. Time was when he had looked suspiciously at his older colleagues in the faculty, opposing with bitter words their tendency to weaken if ever so little the barriers that hedged about the precious parchment. But as he grew older he began to catch glimpses of the fact that education is larger than technicalities, and that the production of "grinds" is not its perfect consummation. He remembered Swift who, as he said of himself, "was stopped of his degree for dullness and insufficiency and at last hardly admitted in a manner little to his credit, which is called in that college '*speciali gratia*'."

The degree of Bachelor of Arts, *Speciali Gratia*— B.A.S.G. Why not? It is true that the teacher has not seen his S.G.'s turn out to be Dean Swifts, but he has seen them play their parts manfully in the world. He has seen them become good business men, good lawyers, and in one or two cases good legislators. If they have not adorned their letters and their speeches with the flowers of rhetoric for which he used to bespeak their admiration, they have—or at least he likes to think so—won a certain fineness of spirit from those spacious humanities about which at the time they seemed to care so little.

And so the teacher has come to view these perennial idlers in the groves of Academe not merely tolerantly but with a measure of expectancy, content to write S.G. after their names in his record, if only they seem to have the making of manly men in them; and always ready to catch, if so it may be, through the cloud of laziness and inertia, a glimpse of that glorious ray which will mark their kinship with the golden idlers—the Scotts and Stevensons —of bygone days.

And if, in addition to the self-directed spirits who are independent of formal "schooling", and the amiably idle who are indifferent to it, there remains a residuum of the incurably ignorant, not even of these need the seeker despair. There is a kind of perfection, an orbicular wholeness about ignorance, sometimes, that is akin to genius itself. They are the leaven of the whole lump, indeed, these indomitable ignoramuses. They are the geniuses in the art of getting things wrong. The student who said that churches promote the mortality of the community, and his fellow who averred that churches are supported by the tribulations of their members had that vatic quality which savage nations are accustomed to recognize and reverence in the weak-minded. The student who said in his ignorance that Leo X sent John Knox to Scotland to sell indulgences was endowed with a finer quality of irony than all the knowledge of the curriculum would have given him. The kings of olden days did well to keep a fool at court.

Not long ago, *The Nation* published a letter from an instructor in a Middle Western college concerning these refreshing ignoramuses—but, alas! the writer of the letter had evidently found no refreshment in them. He had been reading Marlowe's "Hero and Leander" with a class of freshmen. Hellespont suggested Gallipoli. He had asked them where Gallipoli was—and nobody knew. And then, upon these "unfortified brains", as he grimly called them, he made a savage and terrible flank attack:

"What is the capital of Bulgaria? What countries bound Servia? In what country is Salonica? On what sea is Montenegro?

"Who is in command of the French armies? Who is Prime Minister of England?

"Who are Bethman-Hollweg, Poincaré, Venizelos, Briand, von Hindenburg, French, Grey, Viviani?

"Name the rulers of the following countries, giving their titles (i.e., King, Emperor, etc.) : Germany, England, Greece, Servia, Italy, Russia."

And again,—they didn't know.

Ah, me! Of course, they ought to have known. But I wonder, if we (the writer of that letter, and

I) had been freshmen just then, instead of wise teachers—I wonder if we could have passed that examination. My freshman days, I remember, came at the time of the war between Spain and the United States. Could I have passed an equally searching examination on Spain? I shiver at the thought! Nay, could I, even now, suddenly emerge from the rarefied atmosphere of "Hero and Leander", to "bound" Servia? And am I to believe, with this grim Bombarder, that because of the virgin ignorance of these innocent freshmen, the nation is going to the dogs? Honestly, now, Oh, Brother of the Rostrum and Ferule, did we not emerge from a freshman ignorance as comprehensive into the fairly competent citizens that we hope we are to-day? Let us not bombard the unfortified brain too savagely—nay, rather, let us, as all good belligerents should, respect the neutrality of the unfortified brain, and instead of bombarding it and deducing Cassandra prophecies from the resulting devastation, let us give ourselves to a whole-hearted and philosophic enjoyment of the spectacle which it affords.

While, for reasons at which I have already hinted, I have not asked any students for the boundaries of Servia, I *have* asked questions the results of which are numbered among my purest joys. What would the life of the retired and yet adventurous teacher of English literature be without the *Survey Course*? Chaucer, I learn, "lived in the age of Chaucer." "Caedmon lived about the same time as Chaucer, and wrote an early English language. He was a singer and tended towards religion." "Spenser made a translation of the Aenead (*sic*) in which he tells about Helen of Greece who became the wife of Pallas." "Spenser wrote in rhyme but leaned back on the ancients." "Bacon wrote his *Vox Clamantis* and *Speculum Meditantis* on different forms of scientific discovery." "Keats wrote a number of sonnets, both long and short." "Burns comes at the beginning of the nineteenth century. He was an accident."

And what could be more illuminating than the following identification and comment?

> "E'en there before the fatal engine closed
> A wretched sylph too fondly interposed;
> Fate urged the shears and cut the sylph in
>   twain."

"This passage is from Milton's 'Lycidas' which shows the regret and grief Milton feels for the loss of his friend who was drowned. The fatal engine may refer to the two factions in the House of Parliament, although the critics themselves are not certain. The sylph refers to the thread of life. According to the Classics, there are three threads, one which ushers men into the world, one of life, and the other of death. Fate is here personified and cuts the thread of life. He was drowned in the Irish Channel."

Ah, no; let us not bombard these unfortified brains too savagely, or lament too loudly over their "unpreparedness". It is almost, if one but dared to admit it, a matter of regret to see the shades of the prison-house begin to close upon these young geniuses of the perverse, and the splendid vision of their wise blundering fade into the light of common day. "What song the Sirens sang, or what name Achilles assumed when he hid himself among women" were but an unfruitful subject of speculation compared to the thought of what the world would have lost, had Dogberry been put through the mill of Stratford grammar school. "Ignorance is like a delicate exotic fruit," says Oscar Wilde; "touch it and the bloom is gone."

Yes, the splendid follies of the freshman fade into the hopeful zeal of the sophomore and the dogged precision of the junior, and Diogenes trims his lantern and continues his search. It is well to be philosophical, and the geniuses of idleness and ignorance provide their measure of consolation. But the teacher's heart is still strong in the faith that some day a real genius will emerge. And when this sense of the imminence of genius does come, will it be born of the slow and cumulative realization of perfection in all things academic, so that in after years the teacher may repeat of his own pupil those lovely words of Fulke Greville's about Sir Philip Sidney?

"I will report no other wonder than this, that, though I lived with him and knew him from a child, yet I never knew him other than a man; with such staidness of mind, lovely and familiar gravity, as carried grace and reverence above greater years: his talk ever of knowledge, and his very play tending to enrich his mind, so that even his teachers found something in him to observe and learn above that which they had usually read or taught."

Or instead of this slow ripening of many perfections brought to one perfect fruitage, will the advent of the young genius have the kind of abruptness traditional in the type, as of flood gates suddenly released? Will he be a Caedmon, shrinking shyly from the music-makers till the angel touches him? "Then Caedmon meditated all that he had heard and like a clean animal ruminating, turned it into sweetest verse. And his songs were so winsome to hear that his teachers themselves wrote down his words and learned from him."

Symmetrical Sidney or abruptly transmogrified Caedmon—which will it be? Whichever it may be, it is worthy of note that in the words of the venerable Bede and the reverent Greville, there is one thing in common. "His teachers learned of him." Shall the teacher then be wise enough to be gently helpful if so it may be, or humbly docile, if the wings are already strongly spread for flight— or shall the teacher be guilty of some atrocious sort of paranoia, due to the sudden realization of long ungratified desire? There was once a certain Jane Brown, one of the early teachers of Dr. Samuel Johnson, who, when fame came to her old pupil, compiled a spelling book and dedicated it to the universe! *Absit omen!*